Franchise Broker's Handbook

Success Strategies for
Top Producers

Daniel Brunell

President of Dearborn West, LLC
Franchise Development

www.DearbornWest.com

Table of Contents

Introduction

Introduction

This book is a resource for all professional franchise broker types, whether you refer to yourself as a franchise broker, coach, consultant, counselor, guru, etc. This is not intended to be a substitute for franchise broker training. If you are looking for an entry point into the franchise consulting world, I suggest joining one of the quality broker networks available today. There are several solid groups that offer training and tools to help you get started, as well as provide access to product inventory. It is relatively inexpensive, and well worth the investment to learn this business under the supervision of a skilled mentor.

What follows is meant to be continuing education for brokers who wish to increase sales and make operations more efficient. Time is the currency of our business, and it must be spent wisely if you wish to thrive. More than 30 years of recruiting experience has allowed me to develop significant process improvements to the franchise brokerage space. Over the last 15 years, this perspective has helped me succeed in the business of franchisee recruiting. In addition to being a recruiter, I have written extensively about best practices for franchise brokers, and I've served as a training consultant to the industry. I have trained and mentored hundreds of franchise brokers, and I've established strategies to help them achieve more in their businesses. What I have found over the years, is that subtle changes in your operating procedures can yield significant dividends to your bottom line.

In the last decade, the franchise broker profession has emerged as a vital part of the franchise development continuum. Like all outsourced business processes, this saves the franchise customers time, money and institutional energy. However, our service is far more valuable than that of suppliers who simply help reduce costs. We help our customers establish new sources of recurring revenue for their franchise systems. This is our real, and true purpose in the scheme of things, so let me say that again. **We help our customers establish new sources of recurring revenue for their franchise systems.** That is a very big deal. In fact, it is the whole ball game, at least until a franchisor exhausts its build out potential, so we are key players in the big picture. This is important to understand, because if you do not see your role that way, often your customers won't either. You have the capacity to be a critical element to the success of any organization you choose to work with, so you should take what you do very seriously. Just like with all relationships, the manner in which you comport yourself with your clients and candidates, determines how they will treat you. If you see yourself as vital and make positive contributions, they will see you as vital. If you see yourself as simply another vendor, that is how they will view you too.

Our value to the franchise industry is very clear, when you look at the high commissions and robust incentives that the franchisors offer to us. We are also accustomed to franchisors pursuing us to get our time and attention. The best franchise outfits fully understand our value, and desperately want to work with good quality franchise brokers. Because it costs them nothing unless a deal is done, and since we bring in the money to pay our fee, it is a value combination that can't be beat. You should be very proud of what you do, because your contributions have a profound impact on your customer's organization's and on the success of your candidate's endeavors.

My aim is not to throw tomatoes at anyone's process if it works well. This business is very much about style and there is room for multiple approaches. The most popular is the "free coaching" model. The coaching approach is valid, and there are many candidates who respond well to it. If you think the candidate is worthy, and you have the time and patience for this method, it certainly can work. However, I would argue that you are potentially missing a lot of great candidates this way.

Some brokers are more prone to ride herd on their candidates, while others are perhaps a bit too hands off. I think there is a happy medium, and you can get a lot more done if you groom your candidates and customers properly. If you make your focus *recruiting for the companies you like*, instead of trying to find businesses for random candidates, you will make more placements, and probably enjoy this business a lot more too.

I've found it most productive to focus on recruiting current business owners, and senior executives. These are people who are typically pretty confident, and highly self-actualized in their business careers. Also, quite importantly, they tend to have access to investment capital. They are not inclined to fill out forms, have lots of meetings, or listen to you pontificate, but they *are* prone to action. These candidates are high performance types who have the money, skills and personal volition to act. I want my candidates to quickly engage, and be out of my funnel as rapidly as possible, ideally. I really don't want to be dealing with a candidate for six months, and neither do any of my customers. I of course, prefer current business owners over candidates who are contemplating leaving the corporate world. Executives are not the best at making decisions regarding personal lives, and they often don't appreciate the functional roles that support businesses, so they can require a lot of coaching. They are still worthy of your time however, because of the sheer numbers of them in the marketplace.

I want to talk about language, because it has everything to do with how we are perceived. I encourage you to adopt the language of recruiting into your business. There are a lot of reasons for this, but most importantly, it is the most intellectually honest description of what we do. I don't think it's a great idea to present yourself as a buyer's agent, when you are clearly, representing the seller. If you tell people that you are going to work to find them the perfect business for free, it sounds kind of fishy to a lot of folks. The only criticism I have ever seen of our profession has been based on this point, so referring to yourself a recruiter or a franchise development rep, adds a lot of clarity.

The recruiting profession has been around for a very long time, so it already has useful jargon, tools and best practices that translate very well into the franchisee recruiting niche. A franchisee recruiter is very similar to an executive recruiter in that he is working on behalf of a client company to source candidates. The role is to locate, qualify, educate and present the candidate to the client company. Once the introduction has been made, recruiters maintain contact with both parties to make sure they are communicating effectively until they reach an agreement.

There are two key differences between executive and franchisee recruiting. The first is that in executive recruiting, the job order is king, but when recruiting franchisees, the candidate is where the value resides. The second difference is that you get paid much more quickly. In fact, our customers are typically downright excited to pay us, and some of them give us all or most of the franchise fee.

Remember the purpose of the franchise fee, is to cover the acquisition costs of bringing in new franchisees. The best companies understand the new franchisee represents potentially, millions of dollars to them over the life of the agreement. That is why they are in the game, not for franchise fees. Franchising works best when the franchisor and the franchisee succeed together. That necessarily means that the payout for both, is generated by the proceeds from operations, not from fees. It also means that the payout must have long term sustainability. If you currently work with a franchise that is more interested in franchise fees than royalties, you should rethink your relationship.

Referring to yourself as a recruiter is not only a more straightforward approach, but the dynamic with the business seeker is very different. As a recruiter, *you* are the the buyer, and the prospective franchisee is simply a candidate who may, or may not, warrant your time and attention. This may sound like a subtle distinction, but it makes all the difference in the world. Most candidates understand how recruiters work. They understand that your obligation is to source talent to fit the job that you are recruiting for.

Furthermore, casting the prospective buyer as a candidate, helps them understand their appropriate role in the process. We have all talked to the guy who thinks because he is the buyer, he is in control. This is a common misperception, and it needs to be corrected immediately if the candidate is going to be worthy of your time. A quick way to disarm that guy, or extract him from your funnel, is to explain that a franchise is a partnership and he needs to be approved, so he is not in control, they are. He needs to understand that he must successfully interview and win approval from the franchisor's award committee or he won't even have the option to buy that particular franchise.

Once candidates understand that this is much more like interviewing for a job than buying a car, then you have the foundation for a productive relationship. Anything short of that, and you are in for a pride swallowing, miserable experience with an over inflated ego. That is not a fun business to be in, and it is why so many new brokers wash out in their first year.

By approaching this as a recruiting business, you can utilize many of the same first rate tools and best practices created for the executive recruiting industry. Additionally, you can offer a very professional, high-touch service experience that is familiar to your franchise customers, and candidates.

You have also undoubtedly noticed that the terminology in this business is really a jumbled mess. I routinely hear people refer to area development deals as master franchises, and many of our customers refer to candidates as our "clients." The reason they use that language is because many of us do. So for the sake of clarity, when I refer to a client or customer - that is always the one who pays you. We get paid quite well, and I think it is offensive to say to the guy who cuts you checks for 25k, that some potential buyer is your client. Your client is the guy paying you, and the potential buyer, is a candidate. Please be part of the solution and help professionalize our industry by adopting this clearer language in your interactions with franchisors.

Besides language, another factor that is critical to success is your level of commitment. You should reflect on why you chose to become a franchisee recruiter in the first place. For most of us, we chose this profession because of the schedule flexibility, ability to work anywhere, low start up and overhead costs, and a simple operating model. What all of that translates into, is being in a business we can work on our own terms. One that fits around our lives, instead of requiring us to redefine our lives to accommodate the business. This is a best case scenario for most business owners, but the business itself, isn't the goal. The goal is to live the lifestyle you most want to live. For some people that means a 20 hour work week, for others it means buying lots of toys, and for some, it may be about having access to travel or the best education for their children. It doesn't really matter what your desired lifestyle looks like, it only matters that you see your business as your vehicle for accessing it.

Once you start to look at your business as a tool for the achievement of other, more fun and interesting goals, then you have the right mindset to suffer the slings and arrows of the day to day operations part of the business. After all, what isn't worth doing in order to achieve your family's lifestyle goals? When you put it into context, working a recruiting desk is a pretty comfortable way to earn a living.

I have to admit that another handy analogy for our business, is that of a dating service. I feel like a business dating service on a lot of days, and the comparison holds up pretty well. I don't suggest positioning yourself in the market that way, but it can serve as a small joke to break the ice with candidates who are initially, too rigid.

Chapter 1 - Franchise Consulting

There has probably never been a better time to get involved in franchise consulting. There are many drivers that are making this a great time to be a franchisee recruiter, and as the economy expands, it is going to get even better.

The body of talented and experienced management types is growing daily. Many mid-career folks are choosing to become business owners and there is a huge, and growing population of employed people who can't wait to get away from corporate America. We hear it everyday, people are tired of working toward someone else's dream and want to do something for their own families.

Additionally, the structure of large corporate entities has been profoundly altered, and that has changed the employment market substantially. Just thirty years ago, most companies handled everything in house. From conception, to design, through manufacturing, to distribution, everything was done by employees. Not anymore. The old business landscape has shattered into thousands of new pieces. What were once massive companies with many thousands of employees, are now essentially aggregators of services that are performed by a myriad of supplier companies. In turn, many of these suppliers are also aggregators of key services from other companies, as well. The splintering goes on and on, but the net effect, is that these changes have created tremendous opportunities for new supplier companies.

As companies struggle to become more efficient, the number one opportunity for cost savings is typically labor cost. So the trend of hiring fewer workers will continue, which means, ultimately fewer jobs, especially ones that pay six figures or more. This provides the impetus for more and more highly qualified executives to become small business owners every year.

There are lots of young people, more than ever, who are looking to get into business for themselves too. This is supported by the changing nature of academia's treatment of entrepreneurialism. In 1980, only about 300 universities offered courses in entrepreneurship. Now, more than 2500 universities do, and you can even get advanced degrees in entrepreneurship. These schools are responding to immense market demand, and you can see the trend very clearly. People want to be in business for themselves, more than ever, and fortunately, there are more ways to get there than ever before.

We know this is a numbers game, and you have to keep you funnel full. Given the seemingly limitless supply of new candidates who are looking for businesses, we have plenty to choose from, so be selective. Don't give your time to every person who is willing to talk to you. In fact, your role isn't to feed as many candidates into the process as you can. Your role is to eliminate most of the candidates before they get to your customers. Remember, we are here to help our clients save time, money, and headaches. We can only do that by presenting *well-qualified* candidates, who are also a *good match* for the client's type of business. Remember not to confuse someone being qualified, with someone being compatible, for any given business model.

The prime reason our candidates are looking at investing in a franchised business model, is because they want to mitigate the risk involved in starting a business. Most candidates understand that their chances for success will be much better within the framework of a proven model, but they typically do not understand why. The curse of modern times is that there is so much information floating around, but it is not necessarily moored to any basis in fact. I bet most of your candidates think that the value of a franchise comes from its existing brand identity. They reason that if it is a brand people know, then somehow that is all you need for success.

Existing brand awareness in a given market, can of course be a plus, but in no way is it the most important consideration. The business model is the key, and it includes strategies for building your brand locally. McDonald's, Panera Bread and every other mega brand, were unknown quantities in their early days, but smart people who saw the potential, seized on the opportunity to deploy a promising business model in new markets.

If you want to close more deals, you need to help your candidates understand the value of a business model. As you know, a business model is a system for returning economic value. In other words, it is a method for making money. It is a simple concept, but it is difficult to grasp for many. I recently worked with a highly educated candidate who just couldn't get it. This guy had a master's degree in mechanical engineering from MIT and an MBA from the Wharton School at University of Pennsylvania, and *he* didn't even understand the value of a business model. After we discussed an extremely effective b2b business model with average unit volumes of over $6 Million, he said, "Yeah, but what am I really getting besides that?" Clearly, if you can pay someone 40k to teach you how to make 300k every year, there is significant value in that, but this man of letters couldn't process the concept. If a top business school in the US is producing graduates who don't get it, your average candidate can be forgiven for not understanding it either.

Nonetheless, it is crucial to help your candidate see that they are looking for an efficient way to make money, not trying to find a vehicle to further their personal bliss. A franchise is simply a tool, and in the right hands, a tool can create wonderful results. When the candidate views their search as a quest to find a reliable way for them to make money, it removes a lot of the emotion that otherwise clouds their judgment. My whole process is set up in order to help people downplay the emotional elements and intellectualize their decision making. This will always lead to better results.

It is great to be a franchisee recruiter. We help people in very profound ways. We even help many folks come to the conclusion that they do not belong in their own business at all. I am totally ok with this, because it is better for everyone if those folks discover this before they become franchisees. We also sometimes help move people off of really bad ideas that would spell certain financial ruin for them. This is clearly an important public service that we provide, and we do it pro-bono!

Conversely, when we find that perfect fit for a great candidate, we are making a huge difference in the lives of that person, and their family. By helping someone find a business where they can truly thrive, we open up a world of new possibilities. Better vacations, better education for their children, and greater access to the things in life that are most important to them is the result. That's a big deal. A candidate who I placed with a great franchisor a couple of years ago, recently called to tell me that she netted over a million dollars profit in her business last year. That is pretty cool to hear. Be proud of what you do, and be confident. Your value is significant, and even if it isn't obvious to some at first, eventually most candidates realize it.

Chapter 2 - Customer Relationships

Regarding the client side of our business, as you know, there is robust demand for our services, and you should have more clients than you can handle. We are quite fortunate that our client companies are vying for our attention among one another. In order to attract our focus, many offer gifts and incentives, some of them are pretty spectacular too. Of course, the prospect of a higher commission or an incentive award alone, shouldn't drive what you show to a candidate, but it does help keep those companies on your radar. Half of the battle in this business is figuring out which companies to work with, but you should have no problem maintaining a solid list of clients who are eager for your time.

If we are employed in a job, we have to manage our relationships with supervisors, coworkers and customers. Franchisee recruiting is no different. Communication is the key to having good relationships with your customers and candidates, so it is worth the time investment to do it effectively. Keep in mind however, that candidates will come and go, but your client relationships can endure for years. We will be exposed to a wide range of franchises, but instead of many superficial relationships, it is much more productive to forge fewer, but deeper relationships with franchise, and license customers. When you are working closely with a client company, you really get to understand the organization, their specific requirements, and their strategic objectives. This allows you to provide much higher value service.

I can't overstate how big of a plus it is that there is such a huge demand for our services. You can pick and choose which customers you deem worthy of your time. Most businesses have to settle for doing business with the customers who pick them. You should be very selective about whom you spend your time with. I have very high expectations of my customers and when they fall short, I tell them. Being in this business should make you feel confident that you don't have to deal with anything other than top shelf customers. I expect the franchise sales representatives to understand what I do, and how I work. They should be excellent at communicating with you, and your candidate. If you have to constantly chase the franchise sales person to find out what is happening, then you need to train them, or find a client more worthy of your time.

The clients should also have high expectations of you. If you really want to be among the best franchisee recruiters in the world, you should not only be a reliable source of high quality franchise candidates, but you should also be viewed as a knowledgeable resource person. We can easily keep up with the news cycle in the franchise industry if we do a little bit of reading every week. *Franchise Times* is the bellwether publication for the our industry, so if you do nothing else, at least read that, and you can keep up with what's going on in the franchise world. However, if you invest some time in reading *The Wall Street Journal,* you will have a much broader understanding of the overall business marketplace. If you read Entrepreneur, or Inc, you will be more in touch with small business issues, etc.

The IFA puts out a Smart Brief via email. This is free and you can sign up for it at the www.franchise.org website. This is a clipping service that posts articles from around the web that are relevant to franchising. It is another great tool to keep you in touch with the headlines in the industry.
The more you know about franchise opportunities and business in general, the higher your value to both the candidates, and the franchise customers.

Whether you are part of a network or strictly independent, the client companies expect you to do three things well. You must qualify the candidate financially, make sure he has the skills for the job, and make sure he has a reasonable timeframe. Additionally, the clients are even happier if the candidate has a working knowledge of franchising, and is already interested in their business. If we are doing our job well, the skids are greased, and the franchise sales team will have the best odds of closing the deal with your candidate.

Selecting Franchisors to Represent

I have two groups of customers: A-list and everybody else. My focus is always on recruiting for my A-list. However, if a candidate is worthy, and they do not fit with any of my A-list clients, then I will match them to someone in the secondary group. Only franchisors who have the trifecta of a good concept, a good history and a good sales team, make the A-list.

Choosing which companies to work with is one of the most critical elements in a successful franchisee recruiting business. The cruel reality is that there is no substitute for experience. You have to test out the relationship with each franchisor. I routinely come across franchises with really interesting business models, but unfortunately, they have subpar sales people working in franchise development. When I encounter this, I move on. Bad sales people tend to get fired, so if you wait a while, there will be someone new in that role, and you can try to work with the company again at that point.

The fact is that you are working on spec, and you will not be paid unless your franchise customer can close the deals you send them. Some are clearly better than others at running the discovery process and closing deals. It takes time to sort out which companies are the most worthy of your time and attention. These relationships can ebb and flow based on the talent that the franchisor has deployed in their franchise development department, so a great customer relationship can fade quickly when there are personnel changes. You should always be looking for the best in each category that you work with, and be prepared for these to change over time. So stay in the hunt for key companies to represent, because you will have to replace client accounts over time.

It is very important to work with franchisors who respect and understand what we do. This goes beyond the commission scale. There are some customers who pay high commissions, but are still unworthy of your time. Some unsavvy franchisors actually honor the first broker to register a name with them, even if the broker never spoke with the candidate. If a franchisor only cares about who was first to register a name, then they do not deserve you. This is about the worst thing a franchisor can do, because it completely negates the huge value of a quality recruiter's work. The idea of "pre-registering" a candidate is not without merit, but it should only be done after discussing a specific concept with a qualified candidate who is not quite ready to engage yet. Unfortunately, there are poorly trained franchise brokers diminishing our profession by simply registering unqualified leads generated from advertising. This is frustrating to run into, and I encourage you to cross any of the franchisors who accept that kind of schlock, off of your A-list.

Additionally, resale commissions are a very important element when choosing franchisors to work with. If there isn't one in place, get a rep agreement that covers resales, or don't work with the company. I often see franchisors who will pay fees for new unit sales, but have no provision for resales. This is a huge mistake on their part, and it puts them in the absolute last resort category for me (Ok, I guess I have 3 groups of customers!). The bottom line here is that if there is no provision for a resale commission, you run a very real risk of getting cheated out of a placement fee. I have been stung by this before, so I avoid companies with no resale provision. This is what happens. You refer a candidate to ABC franchise. He falls in love. During his validation calls, a local owner says, "I have been thinking about selling. Why don't you buy mine?" The next thing you know, he does buy the resale, and the franchisor says, "Sorry, but you can go ask the seller if he wants to pay you something for your trouble." Of course, they usually won't, and you are shut out with no recourse. Some franchisors may not understand this, and maybe others do not really care, but in either case they are not worthy of your focus, unless you correct the situation.

I can only recall one organization that I've seen with a clawback provision in their commission agreement, but that immediately earned their group a spot at the bottom of my customer list. Franchisor's have strings all over their franchisees, and they do not need us to guarantee their marriage. They should know better than to try and lay off any of their risk on us. Remember, there is no shortage of customers, so stick with the ones who show respect for our contributions.

Another deal killer is when the franchisor keeps you out of the loop regarding what has transpired with your candidate. This must include letting you know immediately if your candidate misses a scheduled appointment. That is critical information to know at the time, not hours, or days later when it may be too late to take corrective action. The people you will have the most fruitful relationships with are the ones who inform you of what happened each time they connect with your candidate. In turn, it is incumbent on you to make sure you share all appropriate feedback with the franchise sales representative too. If we communicate well, we save lots of time for everyone, which means our efficiency is clearly boosted, making it worth the effort.

Additionally, it is imperative that the franchisor be able to respond quickly to territory checks. I want to be presenting businesses to my candidate within 24 hours, so I can't wait a day for a territory check. Some companies are fully automated, so you can check your own territories. That is clearly the fastest scenario, but as long as they turn them around in the same day, I am happy. I also like franchisors who share additional information along with the territory check. The best companies usually provide more information than simply whether the area is available. Often a franchisor will say, "Yes that territory is open, and by the way, our

number one franchisee is next door,"
etc. The more you know about a
market, the better you will be able to
position the opportunity with the
candidate. Unfortunately, you will miss a
lot of this additional information, unless
you actually speak with the franchisor,
so you need to decide which territory
checks warrant a phone call.

It is ok to have a honeymoon period as
you learn how to work with a new
franchisor, but you should have high
expectations of your customers. If you
have to chase the sales person around
for updates, you will grow weary of the
relationship pretty quickly. Besides,
quality organizations, have quality
people, and quality operations. The
franchise development department
should be the most high polish group in
the company. These are the folks who
ask potential franchisees to give them
large sums of money. They should be
very professional, which means they
should have excellent follow through
skills. If anyone seems unprofessional to
you, they will to your candidates too.
You should find a new customer, or

invest the time in training them how to work with your candidates. In any case, you do not want to throw good money after bad, by sending candidates to a company that can't close a deal. You also want to avoid companies that do not reflect your high standards. Nothing good will come from working with a subpar franchisor. Fortunately there are so many companies that are excited to work with you, that you need not waste time on the weaker ones.

Treat your customers with respect, but be candid with them. Give them solid feedback about their process. Tell them what works and what doesn't. Your franchise customers will come to trust you as a key source of market information, so share your insights where applicable. If you are gentle with the feedback, and share in the spirit of continuous improvement, they will appreciate it. The most worthy customers want to understand how to work most effectively with you. We live on commissioned sales, so we need to be vigilant about whom we spend our time with. If your customer doesn't appreciate your input, dump them and get one who does. You get to pick who you want to work with in this business, so always make a conscious effort to do so. Remember the old saying: "You can't soar with eagles, if you scratch with turkeys."

Having worked for many years in franchise development, and especially during my years in the staffing industry, I've witnessed some highly successful sales organizations, and of course, some pretty ineffective ones. The best operations are usually good at two important things; presentation and communication. Most brokers will be showing three or four options, so the candidate will see multiple franchisors from a high level initially, and they will generally look closely at two of those companies. If the candidate has indicated during qualification that he is keen on a particular industry space, i.e., home care, the broker will likely be showing him at least two home care outfits. If the broker doesn't, the candidate will find another one on his own to use as a benchmark, so I usually do it for them. In any case, the candidate will be seeing multiple examples of what a discovery process looks like, so it is important for the franchisor to look as good, or better than their competitors.

The franchisor's presentation really starts with any internet advertising that they do, because it is integrated and geared toward leading people to the website. That is where the company starts to come into focus for most people. It is critical that it shows well, but it is also a huge area of opportunity for the franchisor. If you have sparked any interest, virtually every candidate will visit the franchisor's website immediately following your introduction (and unfortunately, some will do it *during* your presentation). It is imperative that the website be attractive, professional and informative.

If it is not a site entirely dedicated to franchising, there should be a separate tab dedicated to sharing franchise info. Additionally, the website should have a current look and feel. Websites get fancier every year, so the franchisor needs to keep up. Even if the content doesn't change much, it always has to be presented with a fresh looking motif. They must also be fully optimized for mobile devices, and be prepared to adapt to the latest access technology, whatever it may be.

Brochures are almost always electronic these days, so they should be continuously updated to reflect current information. This should be provided to the candidate as quickly as possible, and there should always be a next step built into the franchisor's process. It shouldn't be left to the candidate to control any part of the process, everything should have a clear timeline for completion, and the franchise development staff should take steps to see that the timeline is adhered to. The best companies have sales CRM technology driving their process, so things do not get missed.

The first contact between the candidate and the franchise sales rep should take place on the same day as the referral. Period. If a lead comes in before business hours are over, there should at least be an email sent to the candidate. The key to franchise sales is engagement, and it has to start quickly once we have an interested party. The candidates who are really going to buy something are being tugged in many directions and there is a timestamp on their attention span. When we tee up a great franchise, the candidate's interest is high, but it will drop by the hour until they start to experience the company first hand.

I can start a fire under the candidate, but it will go out unless more fuel is added before the initial flames die down. Even 24 Hours is a long time for a motivated candidate to wait for more info. Candidates get excited about the industry first and the company second, so they are hungry for more info and unfortunately, will look elsewhere if it doesn't start to flow quickly. If the franchisor is slow to connect, the candidate may talk himself out of learning about the concept, because he is absorbing extraneous internet noise while he is waiting.

The booming economy, is a double edged sword, in that we are now competing with a much improved jobs market. It is very competitive for these candidates, so I want to make sure we are staying ahead of the curve. Most candidates are not equipped to judge whether company A or company B has better tools, toys and programs. What they base their decisions on, is the engagement experience and the people they meet during it. I'd really like for my candidates to start seeing how great my franchise customer is on the day of the hand off, if we can make that happen. Smart franchisors will reach out to the candidate to talk then and there, if tenable.

The key is always engagement. The best franchise development staff know that they need to quickly connect with people, and there is no better way than a one on one dialogue by phone. There are myriad distractions for candidates, and once they start shopping, they will have lots of opportunities tugging at their shirt sleeves, so direct engagement is vital. If it is not feasible to have a brief chat at that moment, smart sales people will set an appointment. If a scheduled presentation is set up to review information subsequent to this call, it should happen as soon as possible. Additionally, a presentation meeting shouldn't exceed one hour. This seems to be the sweet spot for candidate meetings. Many quality franchisors have a series of meetings during the discovery process and they end each one with home work or some necessary action required of the candidate. Often information is housed online and password protected, so it is progressively revealed in sequence, as the candidate reads the information that he needs to understand in order to make the subsequent info more meaningful.

As quickly as a candidate can be adequately prepared to formulate intelligent questions about the franchise, he should be given a FDD. Many top franchisors will provide guidance regarding validation calls too. Some candidates may think the franchisor is simply trying to direct them to people who will say nice things, but this is ok. I tell them that there is nothing wrong with getting the thoughts of an unsuccessful franchisee, but there is much more valuable information to be learned from the successful ones. I explain that sometimes it is helpful to give a short list of franchisees to the candidate and tell them to feel free to call at random, but "Here are some people that have similar backgrounds to yours", or "Folks in similar sized markets", or "Here are franchisees at the six month, one year, two year, five year mark", or whatever. The reality is that most candidates get hung up during validation, because they don't know what to do, so guidance helps.

Additionally, all marketing materials, brochures, websites, emails, etc., should have an integrated look and feel to them. This means even the signature line on emails. Everything should look consistent and should have a clean crisp company logo. If the franchisor has skimped on the front facing part of their image, they have probably skimped on a lot of other things too. It is hard to sell franchises in the twenty-first century if they are unwilling to make the appropriate tech investments, and everything begins with the web presence. Make sure the customers you choose to spend your time with are up to date, and understand the value of managing how they appear to candidates.

Obviously, communication between the franchisor and the candidate is key. It should always be friendly, purposeful and professional. While the process needs to be consistent from candidate to candidate, some people like to rely heavily on email, and some will prefer direct communication on the telephone. The manner in which major elements of the discovery process are communicated should not change, but the sales person must be mindful of the fact that some candidates will have quick questions that they prefer to have answered by email. This respects people's time and can be an effective way to keep things moving. Sometimes people will be reluctant to initiate a phone call, because they think it will take too long or they are afraid you will try to pin them down for a decision on something, so email can be a great tool for franchise developers to utilize for greater efficiency.

As long as the candidate always has some home work to do after each call, the process will unfold smoothly. Because it provides a built-in method for knowing if they are on track, it will be very obvious if they are not advancing through the steps. We all tell the candidates that there is no pressure to make a quick decision, but we know the franchisors do not have time to play patty cake with someone for months on end. When the process is adhered to, it gives the candidate an expectation that it will either be a go, or no go, fairly soon.

The communication between the franchisor and the broker can really make or break many deals. Some brokers are very controlling and will want to be a part of every meeting, sitting in with the candidate, but that is the exception. Most brokers will make the referral and expect the franchisor to keep the process going. The candidates typically come to trust the broker and will share information that they won't give to the franchisor, so the broker will usually have helpful insights for the franchisor. The best strategy is for the franchise sales person to either call or email the referring broker every single time the franchisor interfaces with the candidate during the discovery phase. This encourages the broker to share what he knows, and it will also ensure that the broker keeps sending the franchisor candidates. Brokers love franchisors that keep them informed and tend to be very loyal once they find a franchisor that is responsive and can close deals.

As you bring more and more franchisees into a franchise customer, you are influencing the talent base of the organization. When you start to make multiple placements within a franchise system, your touch will be felt by that organization. This will put you on the map within that company, and make you known among senior executives, not just the sales group. You can play a very key role in the expansion of your customer's franchise systems and that can bring rewards beyond all of the commission checks. One of the great things about this business is that you spend all of your time swimming in a stream of opportunity, working with entrepreneurial types, and dynamic, growing, organizations. That makes for a lively work environment, so tap into that energy, and be excited about each day.

How do you decide which companies you should work with? Initially, the list of preferred companies that you develop, builds in several different ways. When you are starting with little or no knowledge of the product inventory, you should begin your list by selecting some companies from popular categories, i.e., food & beverage, automotive, children's, pets, etc. You should have a mix of retail, mobile, home based and business to business type models. The list should also have some fairly low cost options, as well as some mid-range and higher priced options so that you have a pretty good array. Once this list is established, you can work on getting to know each of the companies. You will naturally edit this list as you get to know the target companies. Some will impress you with their professionalism and others will clearly disappoint you with their lack thereof. That is natural and it is a necessary step in cultivating a list of clients who are most worthy of your time.

Because I treat my business as a recruiting agency, I like to focus on a small handful of companies at any given time. I always ask my customers about their top target markets for development. Their answer tells me most of what I need to know about a potential franchise customer. I only recruit for companies that have identified their target markets, because it is a good indicator that they have their act together. I focus on the cities where my customers have overlapping target markets, so that any of the candidates that I generate, can be sent to one of my top customers. This approach is time and cost efficient, because it allows you to kill a few birds with one stone. Also, it signals to the customer that you know what you are doing, and it positions you to make the biggest value impact on their organization.

More than 30 years of experience in the staffing and recruitment space has motivated me to favor b2b service concepts, and specifically staffing franchises. I have many connections throughout the space and a deep understanding of how the industry works. This allows me to recruit more effectively for my preferred customers, and to add value beyond my referrals. If you have specific industry background, or even a strong interest in a specific vertical market, I encourage you to try specialization. Clearly, if you have a good candidate who lands outside of your area of focus, you can still help them find an appropriate business, but this becomes the exception, instead of your primary occupation. You can certainly learn to specialize in any industry you want, so don't let a lack of previous exposure deter you. I learned to be a physician recruiter right out of college, and I certainly had no experience with that!

Specialization has a lot of benefits, but the greatest of these is that you get to become really good at something. You become a subject matter expert that your customers will come to rely on. You have much more control over your process, so you will also find that you are working with a better class of candidates. The candidates with the unique qualifications needed for your industry of focus, will become very easy for you to identify and build rapport with. You will be able to share insights with candidates who can truly appreciate the information you are giving them.

Also, when you specialize, you can customize your lead flow strategies to meet your recruiting objectives. This results in a much more efficient advertising spend that yields more candidates that you can actually use. When you have a very specific candidate in mind, you can build focused referral relationships with entities that can refer exactly the type of person you are trying to recruit. This lowers your frustration factor, because more of the people you talk to every day will be worth your time and energy.

Specialization of course, allows you to build deep relationships with the players in your preferred space. Working closely and bonding with the franchise sales people pays big dividends. They will share a lot more with you and they are more likely to go above and beyond to close your deals. Additionally, by becoming an expert, you may command higher fees in that space, but you will have more control over your earnings too. When you are focused on finding a match for a random stream of candidates, you never really know what you will earn if you are successful. However, if you are focusing on a certain industry, the fees are usually pretty similar, so you can make more realistic revenue predictions based on the number of deals you close.

Chapter 3 - Lead Flow Strategies

Lead generation is an exceptionally important component to this business, so we need to discuss some strategies that go beyond purchased leads. I have shared my own unique brand of guerrilla marketing tactics widely in our industry, and there is no shortage of ideas, but I've found over the years, that most of us simply buy leads. Clearly, you can buy all the leads you want. They are abundant, and there are many suppliers available, but you do need to determine at what point does the cost of the lead exceed its value, and you should always be looking for ways to diversify your approach.

It works well for some recruiters to simply purchase all of their leads, but I think it is wise to always be testing new methods. It is important to keep up with technology, and you should make the best use of the tools available to you. However, don't forget that there are still many low tech solutions that work well and will yield different types of candidates.

Nothing can happen without candidate leads, so you need to develop a strong and reliable flow. The best way to be sure that you are generating enough leads, is to create such a flow that you feel like you almost can't keep up. This formula works whether you are working part time or full time. Lead flow isn't about any specific number of leads, it is simply about having a robust stream of potential candidates to choose from.

When my lead flow is strong, I am much less likely to take on a shaky sounding candidate, but when my lead flow is weak, I find myself stretching and spending time with people I probably shouldn't. This is natural, and it is ok to take a flyer occasionally, but you should avoid these lulls by maintaining adequate lead flow at all times. It is actually far better for some of your leads to die on the vine because you couldn't get to them, than it is to not have enough candidates to call. Consider any waste in your lead flow a cost of doing business, and don't give it any more thought. If you look at your spent leads like stacks of twenty dollar bills you've wasted, this business could get very depressing quickly. Leads are like gas in the tank, and you can't go anywhere without them.

Now that we have established that you need to bury yourself in leads, you might ask, Where do I get the leads? There are abundant sources for leads, and the supply seems almost limitless. Excuse the oversimplification, but there are more than 7.5 billion people on the planet. If only 1% of the population ever bought a franchise, that would mean 75 million potential candidates worldwide. If you are a really busy franchisee recruiter for 20 years, you *might* talk to 100,000 candidates in your career, so you can see the scale. Of course, most of the activity is clustered within the largest economies, so if you work in those countries, you are unlikely to ever run out of leads.

We all know that this is a numbers game, but we can influence our success ratio with a little extra care. The number of leads you work, is simply a measure of how much effort you are expending. What matters is how many quality deals you can maintain in your pipeline. The number will vary based on your own capacity, but I've found that for me, it's about a dozen. If I can keep 12 quality candidates in my funnel at all times, I am in great shape. I always prefer this to having twice as many stretch deals in the pipeline.

There is no silver bullet solution to lead generation. It takes diligence and a little bit of planning to execute a successful, and efficient approach. There are thousands of sources for leads, so you need to adopt a strategy that fits with your budget and time constraints, yet produces enough leads to keep your sales funnel full. The best way to ensure adequate lead flow is to develop multiple channels of leads. A channel is the source of a particular type of lead, such as purchased internet leads, referrals, or business for sale ads. I've found that as long as you have at least three channels producing for you, you will be in good shape. Remember that having three internet lead providers is still only one channel, and even though a lot of people only work purchased leads, you should have alternative channels for best results. Exercise your creativity. Do not limit yourself to the strategies you have heard about. Challenge yourself to come up with new ideas and always be testing the market. You will find that as your creativity increases, your lead buying expenditures will fall.

Channel Selection

Developing effective and diverse lead generation channels is relatively simple, but it takes time. There are many strategies to employ, but you need to pick ones that suit you. The easy way to figure out which channels will serve you best, is to examine your own skill sets and preferences. Are you the type to do presentations to large groups? Are you good at networking? Do you like to write? Do you like to make video presentations? Are you a social media pro? It doesn't really matter which channels you use, as long as your lead flow is sufficient, and you pick channels that you can mine effectively.

Keep in mind that *you*, as a small business owner are essentially the type of candidate that you are looking to engage. Studies suggest that while the average person is exposed to 10,000 or more brand exposures per day, they notice less than 100. Most of this noise is mercifully screened out of our consciousness by our brains, but it can be very instructive to start paying attention to which brand messages actually register with you. Take note of the advertising mediums whose message reaches your consciousness. Record your findings for a week and see what you have. Was it satellite radio or a sign on bus? Was it a flyer on your car? Whatever the sources are, you should consider how you might be able to get your message out using those mediums.

Another very instructive practice is to study what other professionals are doing. Most marketers are trying to reach a similar audience, so the strategies and tactics they employ are worth studying. Think about the professionals you work with. How did your financial planner, or accountant find you? By looking at other professions like; other types of brokers, recruiters, counselors, or realtors, we can learn a lot. Talk to as many other professionals as possible. Ask them how they get new clients (and of course, always explore establishing a referral relationship too).

For instance, by looking closely at what business brokers do to generate potential buyers, we can learn a great deal about where to spend advertising dollars. By learning about how an executive recruiter manages his desk and cultivates candidates, we can bring tremendous efficiencies to what we do. By watching how a realtor handles the dual agency responsibilities, we can learn how to be a better bridge between buyer and seller. Examples are all around us, so start seeking out other professionals whom you can learn from. Keep in mind that the best mentoring relationships are two-way streets. You should always look for ways to repay people's kindness, so don't keep going back to the same well with an empty bucket. You will get more if you give back to those who help you.

What follows is not an attempt to cover every lead generation tactic in detail, or an exhaustive list of all the advertising strategies available to you. I simply want to cover some things that I have had success with. The purpose here is to underscore that you will achieve your best results if you have a multi-channel strategy, and to get you thinking about possibilities.

Types of Leads

Lead generation strategies are either direct or indirect. Direct strategies require personal contact with potential candidates or referral sources. Direct strategies are very powerful and typically produce the highest quality candidates, and often only cost your time to cultivate. Building a referral relationship with a local business attorney would be an example of a direct strategy. Indirect lead strategies rely on a message being received by a potential candidate via some form of media. Purchased internet leads would be an example of an indirect strategy. Indirect lead generation strategies are asymmetrical, so you really don't know quite who will see your message. This can draw in a lot of good candidates, and it can draw in a lot of bad ones too, so be careful to keep your focus on quality leads, not just quantity.

Indirect Lead Strategies

Classified Advertising

In the good old days, most leads came from classified ads running in newspapers and magazines across the country. These ads were generally more solid than the modern internet lead, because people had to have enough personal volition to pick up the phone and call you. This, in and of itself, made the candidate a little more credible from the start.

Classified advertising has certainly changed a lot in the years since, but if you have the patience, you can still find productive channels in print, and in the on-line world. Often a print ad will also include an electronic version in the publication's on-line classifieds too. Classified ads can still work, but keep in mind that they should be short and sweet. As with any advertising that you do for candidates, you only want to put out enough information to elicit a response. That's it. Never try to sell anything in an advertisement, except the invitation to contact you.

Of course, you do not want to mention the name of the client company in the ad, but you do want to be specific about the type business (e.g., dry cleaning or coffee shop). The more specific the ad, the greater response you will get. Remember, lots of candidates start off thinking they know what they are looking for at the beginning of their search, so they respond to specific ideas more than general concepts.

Additionally, where and when you run classified ads, will have a lot to do with your response rates too. I like to run classified ads in trade publications. That way I can target certain professions that typically make good candidates for the various companies I am recruiting for at that time. I use www.newslink.org to find the print publications in cities I am unfamiliar with. If you come up with a great ad that pulls well for you, you can buy bulk space through a company like www.nationwideadvertising.com and run the ad all over the country. This is a strategy that few recruiters employ these days, so you will have less competition for these candidates and could find this to be a productive channel.

Display Ads

Display ads are usually anywhere from 1/8 of a page to a full page advertisement, often for your own business. These can be run in print or online. You can try to persuade people that they need your help by writing a convincing ad that conveys your amazing value in the marketplace. It might even work from time to time, but my advice is to spend that money on something else.

Most people don't understand our value until we directly articulate it to them in a live conversation. Hoping that people will truly understand your value based on the strength of an advertisement is not good strategy. Also, you should be positioning yourself as a recruiter for the franchise industry, instead of someone who wants to help candidates find their dream business. The former will exude credibility, because people understand it and the latter will cause suspicion, because why would you do that for free, again?

Direct Mail

This is another unique way to get in front of potential candidates that most other recruiters will never try. Direct mail isn't cheap, but you can do highly targeted mailing to the exact zip codes that you wish to pull from. The US Post Office has great rates and their are many other vendors supplying this service as well. Most vendors will cut their rates for an introductory trial if you ask, so don't forget to ask. You probably have franchise clients like Money Mailer, or Valpak in your roster, so use that to start a relationship with a franchisee in the area you are targeting. You might even get them to agree to do your mailing at cost, in return for a % of the revenue you generate from their mailings. Be creative!

Another direct mail tactic is to send postcards. I like to use multiple touch points with my "not ready yet" candidates, and a post card is a great way to stand out from the crowd. I send these to certain people who I've spoken with and decided that they were worth keeping in touch with. It is a good alternative to email, which often gets lost in the shuffle. I use www.sendoutcards.com for that purpose. It is cheap and easy to use and the database is highly sortable, so you can send to one person or to groups.

Publishing

If you enjoy writing, it can be a powerful tool for promoting your business. There are myriad on-line, and print publications that would be delighted to publish your well crafted articles. Essentially, all media exist to sell advertising. The more ads they sell, the more content is necessary to fill up a given edition of a publication. Interesting and relevant content is vital to the success of these organizations, and they need lots of it. If they can get it for free, all the better, so the odds of publishing your writing are very good. The best part of writing for third party publications is that it conveys expertise. By simply appearing in print, your credibility soars. This is of course, a double edged sword, because there are so many extremely unqualified people out there, dispensing advice in this way too.

Another angle on publishing that costs little and is simple to maintain, is blogging (or vlogging if you like to appear in videos). A blog is a powerful tool and it is a great way to share your expertise with the world at large. Wordpress is a very popular tool for publishing your own blog, but there are many others. If writing appeals to you, I highly recommend that you at least do a blog, if not writing for business publications directly.

The key thing about blogging is that you need to do it consistently, and at regular intervals for the best results. Familiarity with you is what will cause people to reach out when they are ready for your help. A blog is a commitment, so be sure you are ready for it. Once you start publishing your blog, it's kind of like having a pet bear; you have to feed it regularly or it can be trouble. An inconsistent feed of articles can work against you if your readers come to expect your regular thoughts, and do not get them.

Newsletters are another way to distribute your articles and get your message out to a target group. There are several email marketing tools on-line and if you use a CRM, it may even be an imbedded feature. Like blogging, newsletters are most effective if done at regular intervals. The key here is not to make those intervals too frequent. It is really obnoxious to get daily emails and even weekly is too much. Once per month is a perfect interval for this type of business, but your interval should be determined by how much you have to say. Informative articles with high relevance to budding business owners is what we are going for here. The most compelling content, usually involves key insights, or specific opportunities. If your newsletter is nothing more than another advertisement, it will not hold the reader's attention and it will signal to them that your company is one they can ignore in the future.

Content is King

It is pretty easy to figure out what to write about. The core topics should relate to small business issues or franchising in general. In the normal course of our work day, we are asked a lot of questions. Simply start a log of the questions you get asked most frequently. What's the best franchise? How much does it cost to buy a franchise? Can I get a McDonald's? What do I get for my money? Any of these could be the topic of your blog or newsletter article. My blog articles are typically inspired by a candidate that I am actively working with at the time. I am of course, addressing a wide audience, and the information is broadly applicable, but if the candidate reads my blog, he will likely feel it speaking to him directly. There are often issues that you may cover quite well verbally, but the candidate doesn't seem to really get it. If they can read the same information in an article, it will sometimes stick better.

Another method for finding topics to cover is to simply consider what types of things a potential franchise investor needs to know. How do I find the right fit for me? How do I obtain financing? How do I know what I can afford? These are obviously more advanced questions that allow you to really educate your readers in key areas. You can write a few paragraphs to answer the question and you are ready to publish.

If you get in a pinch, you can always structure your blog as a simple Q&A column. Literally, ask a question and answer it. You only need one or two questions, but pick things with relatively short answers for this tactic. Once you have a body of work that starts to accumulate, take your articles and craft them into an ebook that you can use as a giveaway for candidates. Distribute it through your emails and post it on your website.

Outdoor Media

Most people think of large billboards when they think of outdoor media, but there are many, much less costly ways to get your message out(side). In some communities you can rent space on park benches, or at bus stops, and even on the buses themselves. Another very inexpensive play is to use bandit signs. These are small hand written signs posted around town that call people to action. They must be brief and should look something like this:

Coffee Franchise for Sale
100k and Good Credit Required
951-587-6029

Radio and TV

Radio can be a very effective tool, but it can be very expensive in major markets. It is accessible, but you need to develop a relationship with an advertising sales person. Tell them what you can afford for a trial and what you spend in a year on advertising. They will often have special promotions and discounted pricing for new customers, so alway ask. Ask when the next promotion is coming up. They will often figure out a way for you to work with them, especially in smaller radio markets.

Network television is typically out of reach, but there are often bargains in cable tv advertising. Further, if you like the idea of hosting your own show, it is easy to create on-line programs now. Additionally, you could create your own YouTube sensation. If you establish a body of work on YouTube and link those videos to your website, you will add jet fuel to your search rankings.

Internet Leads

By far, the most popular source of leads in our business are the internet search portals. These websites catalogue information about various franchises and offer further details to people in exchange for their contact information. The candidates arrive at these portals based on pay per click advertising and aggressive search engine optimization strategies. Some of the lead vendors offer specific leads for specific brands. Others offer low cost, but completely random leads and others still, offer higher priced leads that have been touched by a screener before they come to you. Additionally, you can buy leads for people who are asking for a free consultation with a franchisee recruiter. There are variations on these themes, but essentially the internet leads are relatively cheap and abundant, so they can be instrumental in ensuring that you always have leads to call.

You should always have some component of your marketing spend dedicated to producing internet leads. Initially, this should be the bulk of your marketing budget, but as you grow your channels, and incorporate other strategies, you can migrate some of this spending into other tactics. Keep in mind that vendor selection can take time, and sometimes, a once productive vendor can lose its luster, so keep testing the market. Remember to negotiate on price, never accept the retail rates first quoted to you. They can, and usually will do better, if you just ask. Tell them to give you a reason to try them out.

There are some great lead vendors who fly under the radar, but most of the ones you will come to rely on are in the Top 15 lead vendor report that is put out quarterly by the Franchise Benchmark organization. These are the bigger companies who invest more to stake out the best territory on the internet, so they get the lion's share of the traffic. If you wish to test the strength of any advertising website, try www.trafficestimate.com. You can get a free traffic estimate to see how many unique visitors they have each month, along with some other interesting data points. It is a handy tool once you get used to using it.

A simple way to see which portals are the easiest to find and therefore ostensibly most productive, is to try typing in a few common keywords used in searching for franchises (e.g., best franchises or franchise opportunities). The portals that come up on page one are the most visible, so they will naturally, receive the most traffic.

I cannot definitively say that you should use raw leads or that pre-screened leads are really the way to go. I think they can both work well, but it is really a matter of preference. I like controlling my message very tightly from beginning to end with my candidates, so if an autoresponder goes out, it is one that I have written. Additionally, I do like the prescreened leads and they are worth it for the right price, but I have always been comfortable kissing my own toads too. It doesn't take long to figure out if you shouldn't work with most candidates and it can often save you a fair amount of money if you have good flow, and don't mind doing the screening yourself.

Other On-line Sources

We talked about classified ads, but there are seemingly endless other ways to get your message out on the internet. There are local advertising sites in most cities and they are often very inexpensive. These websites are usually promoting local fine dining, or the arts, so they tend to be patronized by educated folks with some means. This is obviously a good target audience for us, so find a message that plays well and get it in front of that crowd.

Classified websites like Craigslist, or Kijiji, can be a very cost effective way to get your message out. The ads are cheap or free, but they can die after only a week, and it takes some time to keep a fresh presence, but again the price is right. There are many other "free" sites for classified ads, but keep in mind that most of the smaller ones will only result in you being put on spam lists, so utilize alternate emails for these purposes, not your main email address.

Business for Sale Websites

There are as many business for sale sites as there are web portals, but again, you can see who the big guys are just by trying some "business for sale" keyword searches. You have clients with resale units, so just pick one that looks halfway decent and create a listing at one of the sites like www.BizBuySell.com. This strategy will give you access to a different slice of the marketplace than you will get from portal leads. You will get a lot more current business owners than you will corporate expatriates, and they are much easier to work with. Of course, most of the respondents will be interested in hearing about the specific listing that you posted, but once you explain what you do, you can usually gain their consent to do a broader search on their behalf. Again, people don't like to leave stones unturned!

Pay per Click

You can establish your own pay per click lead generation strategy, but quite frankly if this isn't already an area of expertise for you, I would leave it to the professional lead generators. It is typically more cost efficient to purchase leads from the vendors instead of trying to compete with them on their turf. There are lots of resources, and droves of free information available on the web if you would like to learn the intricacies of pay per click, but here are a few points to keep in mind:

- It can be tricky and costly, but you can get immediate results.
- Only target markets where you need candidates.
- Make your keywords specific, and block negative clicks.

- You must absolutely have a great landing page that quickly captures the attention of the visitor.
- Consider offering a free eBook to visitors. You can then capture contact information, and improve the "stickiness" of your site.
- Be careful to set realistic budgets for your campaigns.
- Expect it to cost you upwards of $100 for each new candidate that you put into the pipeline.
- The later in the week your ads run, the less responses they will pull.
- Also, the last two weeks of the month are softer in terms of volume, so traffic is lower, but so is the cost per candidate typically.
- Carefully consider the time, energy and expense involved to determine if this is worthwhile for your business.

Associated Website Info

Another tool for generating candidates, are websites that give away free information that aspiring business owners might find interesting. It is very simple and inexpensive to create a website. You need to either create or collect enough information for a white paper on some area of relevance like business plan writing, small business funding solutions, 401k conversions or business coaching, etc. Anyone who visits the site can download the free information, but only after they supply their contact information. Promoting the site takes some creativity, but simply attaching it to newsletters, emails and your website can go a long way to making this a productive method.

Search Engine Optimization

If you are going to promote any websites for the purpose of lead generation, I highly recommend finding a local SEO guy. It is not that expensive to pay someone monthly to keep your landing page at the top of the search results. If you do hire an SEO consultant, it doesn't hurt if he has worked with a recruiter before, but you should demand that you are the only one he is working with at the time. Also don't forget to ad a blog or videos to your website as these boost the rankings considerably. The key here is to never stop innovating. The landscape is changing rapidly on the internet, so it takes some work to keep up.

Social Media

Social media has become all the rage these days and it can be a productive business tool, but it needs to suit you in order to be effective. I don't want to put too much emphasis on age, but social media seems to play best with the younger generation. We in the over 50 crowd, may not be as comfortable with this platform. We may even prefer to net the older candidates who come with the more traditional lead generation strategies. However, Facebook is mostly for the over forty crowd, so there are definitely opportunities. I am not going to pretend that I know all about social media. I am currently testing out some new social media advertising, and it is far from obvious that it will be a big hit at this point, so I'll update the next edition of this book with my findings. Nonetheless, there are a great deal of resources available for free on the web if you are interested in pursuing a social media strategy, so I will just share a few thoughts here.

There are many different social media sites and they range from truly social, like Facebook to professional, like LinkedIn. There are so many social media tools that there are even social media management applications like Hootsuite, to help you coordinate your efforts. Tech savvy franchisee recruiters are figuring out how to make social media work optimally for them, so it is an area of opportunity for anyone who is interested in developing a strategy. Our business is targeting a fairly specific slice of the population, so if you can craft your message well and get it in front of the right people, this channel holds a lot of promise.

A note on social media strategy. Don't simply advertise. It is best to join groups relevant to your business, such as those on LinkedIn or Quora.com, and engage in the conversations. By joining in and offering answers to the questions people ask, you can distinguish yourself as an expert on franchising within the group. Members will eventually start to ask you questions directly and then as appropriate, you can offer more direct help to anyone in the market for a business. There are dozens of social media marketing agencies who can create and execute your on-line efforts if you wish to develop this channel. You are probably hearing from many of them regularly via email blasts.

Again, if you like to make videos, be a Youtube sensation, and link your topically relevant vlogs to your website. In any case, the technology is available to reach people in a big way. If it appeals to you, and you really embrace social media, it has a lot of potential.

Crowd Sourcing

This is an old concept with a new name that is substantially more effective now with modern communications technology. Crowd sourcing is essentially using the power of groups to solve problems. Posing a question to your group of connections on Facebook or LinkedIn is an example of crowd sourcing. Additionally, there are now websites dedicated to crowd sourcing certain issues. There is one called leadvine.com that is all about sourcing leads, and there are others that range from getting water to rural African villages, to sourcing bids for engineering projects. Cooperation and collaboration are powerful business tools, so search for people and entities where you can create mutual benefit.

Recycling

Since the goal is to bury yourself in leads, you can rack up a lot of old leads fairly quickly. A good way to utilize these not quite hot leads is to add them to an email marketing campaign like your newsletter, so they continue to get a touch from you. Whether you have email marketing built into your CRM, use an ASP, or use software, there are rules regarding permission, so be careful not to be a spammer. If you have colleagues you enjoy working with, by all means try swapping some old leads. Sometimes candidates aren't ready, or act stupidly, or feel bad about never responding to you, so they will avoid you. If you and another broker share leads that could have merit, but just never panned out for you, you will both come up with some placable candidates for free.

Direct Lead Generation

Growing a referral base for your business can improve your results and drive down your operating expenses. You can save money, but it definitely takes time to cultivate sources. The great thing about referrals, is that a lot of screening has already taken place. Someone respects both you, and the candidate enough to put the the two of you together, so there is credibility for both parties right out of the gate.

It is worthwhile to develop some referral channels that suit you, because the quality of the candidates is so high. Internet leads often represent a 100 to 1 success ratio, but my ratio of leads to deals with personal referrals is about 4 to 1. So for every four referrals, I can count on a deal occurring. That math works really well, and there are a lot of ways to start slowly building relationships, so don't miss out on this.

Public Relations Firms

There are a lot of talented people who have left large PR firms to start their own shops, closer to where they live. This means that you can often find big agency talent in smaller local firms, with reasonable rates. When you find a good PR representative, tell them what you do and how it works, so they understand that you need to source business buyer candidates. Make sure that you agree on what the expectations are and what the fees per month will be. Set specific goals for them to obtain, like getting you two speaking gigs per month or gaining radio/TV exposure, etc. If the goals are clearly defined, you will both be much happier with your relationship.

Franchise Buying Seminars

There is tremendous public interest in franchise investing, and there are a lot of people who will gladly attend a free informational session. These events can yield great candidates, not just leads, so if you like presenting to groups, this can be a very effective strategy. The key is to set it up at a quality venue and promote it properly. This could be at a hotel, the conference room at the local chamber of commerce, or at an outplacement center, among other venues. Promoting the event in the local paper is a good way to boost attendance, but if you book it with an organization, like the Chamber of Commerce, they may promote the event for you.

Your key franchise customers may be interested in partnering with you on these types of events. They will often pay for the room and help promote the event in return for a spot in the program to present their franchise opportunity to the crowd. Just make sure to agree in advance how any candidates generated by the event will be handled.

A lunch and learn at a restaurant can be very productive. Especially if you do it in conjunction with the Small Business Development Council (SBDC) or Service Core of Retired Executives (SCORE) or any similar group, because they not only help promote the event, but they give it more credibility with the attendees. Require an RSVP, so the group is manageable, but aim to treat about ten people to lunch at Sizzler (or some buffet type place) and teach them about investing in the franchise industry.

Just remember, the presentation has to be about buying a franchise, not an hour long commercial for your business. The attendees must have some tangible takeaways from your speech. So make sure you are teaching the attendees things that they can use and helping them gain some insight into the process of investing in a franchise.

Trade Shows and Job Fairs

Once upon a time, setting up booths at trade shows was an indispensable method for attracting new franchisees. These events can certainly still bear fruit, but they can be expensive, so you need to pick your battles wisely if you wish to employ this strategy. I would recommend that you attend as many franchise and business opportunity trade shows as you can, but do it as an attendee, not an exhibitor. These are great places to meet your franchise customers in person, and do some bonding. You may even land a new candidate or two, but don't make it about recruiting, make it about getting to know your current customers. When I went to my first Franchise Expo as franchisee recruiter (over 15 years ago now), half of the franchise sales people in the room had never even heard of franchise brokers. It is very different now, to say the least, so if you see concepts that you like, you can add some new customers while you are there too.

The one thing that I wouldn't recommend is setting up a booth at the franchise show. If you want to sell the franchise consulting business opportunity, that is one thing, but setting up a booth to recruit candidates for placement with client companies, puts you in direct competition with your own customers, at the same event. Not a good idea. Let them have the day. Besides, you look pretty uninteresting next to spokesmodels handing out free smoothies, or pizza.

There are many other, non-franchise shows that could be productive for you to field a booth if the price fits your budget. Automotive shows and home shows are great places to put related business opportunities in front of people who are already interested in those realms. Often you will have little competition in such environments and will get a greater share of the attendee traffic.

Job fairs are coming back with the rising economy and if you can find executive level venues, it can yield great results.

There are a lot of mid-career management types who have lost their jobs or are afraid of losing them. The older you are and the further past age 50 that you are, the dimmer your job prospects are going to be. Many of these older execs feel humiliated with the whole job fair experience. Finding a booth that offers hope of emancipation from all of the indignities of the modern career, is like an oasis in the desert. Just remember that most of the people attending need a job, not a business, but it is worth sorting through them, because the best candidates are often the ones who didn't know they needed your help to begin with.

Networking

Everyone talks about the power of networking for good reason, it works. In our business, we can build a national network of referral sources if we are willing to invest the time. The first step in developing a referral business is to tap into your existing network. Consider your friends, neighbors, relatives, business contacts, etc. These folks could be a terrific source if you let them. Craft a letter and send it out to everyone. Make it simple and soft. Don't make it an aggressive shakedown for leads. Simply, let people know what you do and who you can help. You probably have a few referrals waiting for you in this group if you haven't done this yet.

Developing Referral Sources

Getting referrals from family and friends is great, but if you really want to develop a strong referral business, you need to build relationships with other professionals. The best way to open the door to a new referral relationship is to offer to *send* referrals. We are in a very unique business, and we are routinely in a position to send referrals to others. Think about all of the things a new business owner may need; a lawyer, an accountant, an insurance agent, an architect, a general contractor, equipment leasing guys, lenders, etc. All of these people would appreciate your referrals, and at the same time, you are not only helping the candidate, but you are helping to keep the process moving forward.

Attorney's can be a great source of referrals and I have had good results in particular with immigration, business, and some estate & trust practices. CPAs are also excellent sources for candidates. The CPAs have clients who own businesses, and they often know who is ready to buy, or sell. Another great thing about referrals from law offices and CPAs, is that they cannot ethically, accept any payment for referring their own clients to you. That means that you operate under a system of generalized reciprocity, whereby they send you referrals and you send them referrals, no fees are paid.

Some other productive relationships to target would be with financial planners, land developers, SCORE, SBDC, city planners, or business and career coaches. Commercial realtors are good to know as well. One tactic I've used with commercial realtors is to put up a sign in their retail spaces that says "Coffee shop owner wanted for this space" or something similar. Often the simple suggestion of what the space could be, is enough to motivate someone to actually call and ask about it.

You can develop a national network with these types of people by calling them up and talking to them about how your business can help them directly by sending them referrals, or help their clients by finding them safe business investments. As you recruit in specific markets for your favorite customers, spend a little time getting to know the marketplace. If you are doing a lot of recruiting in Cleveland, then spend some time calling some attorneys and CPAs in the area. They could make your job a lot easier. The important point here is to target smaller firms. The 200 attorney, white-shoe law firm downtown, is not interested in your referrals, but the firms with 1 to 4 attorneys, will be all ears when you say you can send them referrals.

You can of course, also meet these folks through involvement in professional, civic, and social organizations in your local community. In any case, the key to developing these relationships is having regular interaction with them. The best way to do this is by sending them referrals or helping them achieve their goals in some way. In our business, the more referrals we make, the more we get back, so if you are not casting any bread on the waters, don't expect to get any back.

Outplacement Groups

Outplacement groups provide job search and transition services to employees that have been laid off. The services are often included in severance packages and are paid for by the downsizing employer. These services are also offered on a retail level directly to the jobseeker, but the corporate sponsored ones are usually what we want. There are some big players in this space, like Right Management and Lee Hecht Harrison, but there are many smaller firms in most markets too. Call up some centers in the market where you are working and tell them that you would love to help any of their clients who are interested in business ownership. Tell them you can provide free franchise information or counseling for their clients. Offer to come in once a week, or once a month, to present a seminar for transitioning execs on how to invest in a franchise.

Outplacement groups charge a fair amount of money for their services and the more they can offer the client the better, so if they do not already have a relationship with a franchisee recruiter, they will want one. If you are good at developing these, you could potentially be busy all of the time, just from these leads. Of course, I recommend multiple channels, but this can be a pretty lucrative one. I like to use www.superpages.com to find local outplacement groups.

Military Recruitment

Discharge centers can be an excellent connection for your business, so get to know discharge staff at military bases to establish connections to retiring personnel. A good way to find guys who work on the discharge side, is to talk to military recruiters for each branch. It is the same mission, so these guys cycle through from recruiting, to discharge responsibilities during the course of their careers. They can help make connections for you and it is always better to start with a name.

As you know, franchisors love military veterans. They know that armed services personnel are well trained and very capable of following specific procedures. Also, they expect to win, and they are often hungry to start earning a better income. We as a society, cannot do enough for our veterans, and helping them is especially rewarding, so I encourage you to work with as many veterans as you can.

Additionally, franchisors participating in the VetFran program offer incentives to all armed services veterans, making hundred's of franchises more attainable for service members. This can be a great way to help those families who serve our country in a very profound manner. Any veterans can be good candidates, but the retiring, career veterans with some rank, are highly prized by the franchisors, so they tend to be excellent candidates to work with.

Executive Recruiters

I always recommend that franchisee recruiters be well connected with management recruiters. In fact, the more, the merrier. These relationships can be very productive in that both sides routinely come across candidates that would be better suited for either a job, or a business. Management recruiters archive every resume that crosses their desk. Even though most recruiters specialize, they save every resume they receive and they index them for easy retrieval. This database can be very valuable if you let the recruiter know that you can help monetize that inventory.

In management recruiting, a job order is the basis for action. So, instead of simply saying "If you run across a candidate with…", I give them the equivalent of a job order. I'll be quite specific and give them the profile of the candidate I am looking to find. In their world, everything is a 50/50 split when they collaborate, so I will offer up to 50% in these situations. This is an exception that I only make with recruiters, because of the special nature of the relationship and how productive it can be (I would otherwise, not recommend paying more than 20% in referral fees). You will make friends very quickly once you start paying out referral fees, so you will not find it hard to develop a productive network.

Networking Groups

There are several networking groups like BNI or LeTip, and these can be productive if they have a good group of members, but sometimes they can take up a lot of your time too. The weekly meetings themselves aren't bad, but the ancillary meetings with all of the group members who want to have coffee dates, can get cumbersome. I like smaller groups of people who all work with business owners in some way. My first affinity group had a business lawyer, an accountant, a marketing person, a business insurance agent, a lender and me. This was perfect for passing referrals back and forth. We ultimately published a quarterly newsletter as a way to get each other in front of our respective client groups. Be careful to pick members who have the same values and ethics as you!

Franchisor Customers

The franchises that we work with receive lots of leads. Most of these leads will not be a fit for that particular franchise. Once you have developed a good relationship with a franchisor, ask them about their dead leads. See if they would be willing to share them with you. Some franchisors have really tight legal restraints and will not do this, but many younger, up and coming franchises will be happy to share. I like to offer an incentive back to the company for their leads that become placements. Just make sure that you are compensating the company directly, and not the sales person.

Master Franchisees

An excellent way to leverage franchisor relationships is to align with master franchisees. These folks typically have large cash investments on the line, so they are very open to working with brokers. In fact, that is how most of them get their units sold, so this is a receptive audience. You can usually get a dual benefit from these relationships in that you can not only ask them for leads, but you can also help sell their units. I like to offer them some incentive, such as 10 or 20% of any placements made off of their leads. This is a tremendously attractive deal for a master franchisee, because they can convert their dead leads from an unrecoverable cost, to a potential source of revenue.

Local Franchisees

Another thing that I like to do, has paid dividends over the years. As long as it is not too busy when I go into a retail franchise, I'll start a conversation with anyone who looks like they might be the owner. They are usually easy to spot, because they are typically polishing or straightening something. I'll ask them if it is their shop, and if they say yes, I'll ask how they found the opportunity. More often than not these days, they will say that they had help from a broker. This is mostly just to give them something easy to talk about. After that, I ask if they ever get people who ask them how to get one of these franchises. They will say yes, because it happens a lot. Ask them if they are offered any incentives from the franchisor for referring candidates. Very often, they say no. At this point, I give them some of my business cards and tell them that I will pay them $500 for every successful referral they send me. It is a no brainer for the shop owner. He not only has people who show up in his shop asking him about franchises, but many of his friends will also be potential referrals too. It is kind of funny, but frequently the friends and families of people who own a franchise, somehow think that that person must be an expert on franchising. This causes misguided folks to inundate them with questions about bizarre franchises, and harebrained schemes. Most of these franchisees would be delighted to send their curious friends your way.

Emerging Franchisors

There are many emerging franchises that could be worth aligning with, especially if you can get a twofold benefit. If the company seems like they have strong leadership, a great concept, and a solid business model, you may be able to overcome the fact that they are a new franchise. A lot of young franchisors have limited staff, and often the founder is tasked with selling franchises and running the operations part of the business too. Usually, the only thing they know how to do, is to buy internet leads. Unless they are previously experienced, these guys are typically ill prepared to properly qualify candidates, so they spend too much time with anyone who comes along. This is a very wasteful and frustrating approach. I tell these owners that I would be happy to be their initial screener for all of the leads that they are buying. This way they can get the most out of their leads and only spend their time talking to credible candidates. They also get a highly experienced franchisee recruiter who is willing to work on spec. This is huge, because they could never afford to hire you, but in this case they still get to benefit from your expertise. In return, they pay the standard recruiting fee when they sell a franchise from any leads that you touch, and you pay them a small referral fee if you place any of leads that were not a fit for their company, elsewhere. This can be a great arrangement, but you will naturally outgrow it as the franchise expands and gains momentum.

Organizations

Joining any group of people can exponentially increase your reach. There are endless networking, professional and social groups that you can join. Most of these associations can help your business if you ask folks for referrals. The thing to keep in mind is that you need to be able to glean enough benefit from your involvement to make it worthwhile time wise. You'll need to establish what that means to you, but remember time is money, and you never stop spending it, so make it count.

The key to getting the most out of an organizational affiliation is to get involved beyond the basic member level. Join a committee, or get involved in the leadership of the group. Only when you donate time beyond simply attending meetings, will you really start to reap the rewards of the relationships you form in these groups. When you volunteer your time, and energy to the cause, you will build relationships with others who are doing the same thing. Once people get to know you, and understand your value, they will start sending you referrals.

It doesn't matter if it is the local chamber of commerce or a bowling league. The thing to remember when interacting with the group is that you must place the mission of the organization first, and your business interests second. Additionally, follow the rules of effective networking and basic manners. Don't prattle on about your business without sincerely trying to understand the other person's business too. Everyone dislikes when people do this. It is rude and more harmful than missing the meeting in the first place, so don't make that mistake! If you are unsure about how to work the room at a networking event, there are droves of books and articles on the subject, so it is not hard to master with a little reading and some practice.

Candidates as Referral Sources

Your candidates can be a very good source of leads, so treat them accordingly. The candidates that you place in new businesses are obvious sources of referrals, but you need to ask. Never assume that they know you want their referrals. Most humans are not sales people, so they do not really appreciate the value of referrals, and they are not trained to give them. Additionally, the folks you place in a new business are going to be exceedingly busy for the next year or so, and you will not likely be at the top of their mind. This is a good reason to ask them for referrals through your newsletter, so they get a regular reminder.

Another class of candidates is even better for obtaining referrals. The candidates that you spend a great deal of time with only to prove out that they do not belong in business ownership at all. These folks are often sensitive to the fact that they have taken a great deal of your time, and they realize that you have taught them a great deal, and potentially saved them from trashing their lifesavings, but they also know that you will not be paid. They usually say something like, "If there is ever anything I can do for you..." I always take that opportunity to ask them for referrals. Most folks appreciate the opportunity to repay your kindness and will proactively, seek referrals for you, but you have to ask!

In addition to your newsletter, you can ask for referrals in targeted post card mailings, on your emails or any other communications for that matter (some recruiters even ask for referrals on their outgoing voicemail messages). It's always a good idea to ask, so don't hesitate. Remember, if you don't ask, you don't get.

Consideration for Referrals

The great thing about building a referral network for your business is that the cost of the referral is low, but the caliber of the candidate is often high. This makes generating referrals worthy of your time, because if you pay anything for the lead, it is only after you have earned a fee. My standard referral fee is $500, but I'll pay more to other professionals who send me high caliber candidates, and I'll go up to half with recruiters, as we discussed earlier.

I get a lot of referrals from attorneys and CPAs, which is great, because they cost nothing, but the key here is generalized reciprocity, instead of direct. What this means is that you cannot offer any direct compensation for referrals, but you can respond in kind, by referring candidates to them. These are among my most productive referral relationships and I go out of my way to send candidates to them regularly.

The secret to establishing a great referral business is simply to spend some time each week, sending referrals out to other professionals. Remember, every aspiring business owner can benefit from referred professional resources of all kinds. Get to know people in professions that support small businesses in the markets where you work most often, and build your list. Lawyers, accountants, general contractors, credit card processors, lenders, insurance brokers, etc, are all necessary contacts for business owners. It is great when someone needs a competent franchise attorney and you can send them a list with multiple options to choose from. This kind of proactive referral strategy will in turn, generate a flow of referrals to mercifully balance out your internet leads. If you are always looking to connect the dots in your relationships, and truly desire to help others, you will definitely see an increase in your referral business.

Also, keep in mind that corporate gifts can be very useful tools as well. Sometimes a well placed bottle of wine or scotch whiskey can mean a lot to your referral source. Maybe an occasional lunch or a round of golf? Just look at your relationships and resolve to figure out what type of kindness you would like to pay given the relationship, and then pay it!

Lead Tracking

It is undeniably the 21st century, and there are many technology tools that will help you run your practice. A good CRM system is an excellent tool. It can increase your reach and save you a great deal of time every day. Having said that, what ever you use to manage your workflow, it needs to be something that is easy for you to use. Some may find a simple spreadsheet or a paper system works well for them. That's ok! What we are after is an efficient and organized process that allows us to retrieve information quickly. It really doesn't matter how you do it, as long as it works, and you have a system that saves you time, instead of costing you time. Whether you use a CRM or you work with paper files, it is critical that you are highly organized. Again, being able to retrieve information quickly is important, so pick a system that works for you and use it faithfully.

There are a number of great CRM tools available to franchisee recruiters. If you are tech savvy and can type, I recommend that you use one of them. It makes things a lot easier and you can use the system to really squeeze the most out of every lead. They include pre-designed email communications, drip feed campaigns and excellent sorting and retrieval of candidate information. Many of these programs will also create the candidate file automatically and populate all of the basic fields, so you don't have to type all of that information yourself. If you are not the best typist or you don't like to rely on electronic data retrieval, an automated CRM may not be for you. The good news is that you can still operate this business mostly on an analog basis.

When I started in the early 2000's, there were precious few tools available for franchisee recruiters, so I set up a hybrid system that I still use today. When considering your strategy for staying organized, keep in mind that your relationships with candidates are relatively short lived, but your relationships with the franchise customers will build over several years. This means that you need a system that accommodates your very different needs for both constituencies. You can be all paper or you can set up a combination of paper augmented with technology.

My simple system uses one red file folder to hold all of my leads. Every lead that I receive, irrespective of source, is either printed or written on a piece of paper. All of these leads reside in my red folder while I am trying to reach them. Once a lead has been qualified, if they become a candidate, they get their own green file folder. This green folder is where I keep all of the notes on that candidate until he is placed or flushed out of the process. If a candidate is ruled out, or never reached, then the lead goes into the dead file (which may or may not be later entered into your newsletter database or may be resurrected and called again down the road). I also keep blue file folders on my client companies. I write the names and dates of every referral to that company right on the file jacket. I keep any notes on the business in these blue files for quick retrieval. I of course, use software for email, calendar and franchisor contacts, but candidates are mostly paper files that come and go rapidly. The only thing I have to key in, is the candidate's email address if I add them to my newsletter.

Again, the key here is to pick a system that fits your skills and comfort level. Whatever you do, it is important that you settle on a lead tracking system and an operating procedure that you can administer simply, without wasting too much time. Remember, at least 80% of your time should be spent speaking to humans. If you spend more than 20% of your time on administration, rethink your approach! Whether you use a fancy

CRM program, paper, or a spreadsheet, it is most important to be able to see where your deals are coming from (or not coming from) by lead source. Lead generation is never settled. You must always be testing the market and trying new things, just make sure you have a way to evaluate the things that you try, so you can operate most cost effectively.

Closing Thoughts on Lead Generation

The truth about lead generation, as you can see, is that there are endless avenues to attract leads. You don't need to use all of them, but you need to pick a few channels that work well for you, and then run with them. Track your results, and periodically re-evaluate your sources. Make changes where necessary, and don't be afraid to try new things. Just stick within your budget guidelines, and don't let advertising sales people coax you into trying anything outside your comfort level. Remember, it is better to have some of your leads die on the vine, than to not have enough. If you keep yourself buried in leads, and always feel like you can barely keep up, you are doing it right.

We are only limited by our own creativity. Challenge yourself to try new ideas, think about what relationships you have already that you can leverage, and ask yourself "What am I willing to do to create new relationships?". I also encourage you to share ideas with your colleagues. Just like referrals, when you share good ideas with your colleagues, they will start to do the same with you, and in the long run, you will gain more than you give. If you simply develop the habit of helping others get what they want, you will be surprised, frequently, by how often new referrals appear. It always makes my day when I get a really good referral. It is usually a nice surprise too, because for some reason, they often line up well with whatever I am working on at the time.

Chapter 4 - Qualifying Candidates

Remember, our primary function as franchisee recruiters, is to attract qualified talent for our customers, not to find businesses for candidates. If the candidate understands this is your primary objective, you will be way ahead of the game. It is important to always keep our focus on our core mission of serving the customer, with the understanding that the candidate is the key to that objective. Intuition is an important tool when it comes to evaluating a candidate's readiness to become a franchisee. If something is telling you they are not a great candidate, they probably are not. Listen to your gut feelings. As you become more and more experienced, your intuition will become more and more reliable. Remember, if a candidate looks shaky to you, he will look even worse to your franchise customer.

While serving our clients, we can help candidates in profound ways, but our role is not to help them find personal bliss. Too many folks are obsessed with the pursuit of their own joy, instead of the potential of the business. I am amazed by how many candidates are looking for an ideal scenario, instead of a business opportunity. I am all for having your cake, and eating it too, but people need to be realistic, and flexible. That is why your initial qualifying call should establish that *your* objectives are at least as important to you, as the *candidate's* objectives are to them. If they understand that they are a candidate, not a buyer, and that your goals lie in parallel with theirs, then you can have a productive relationship.

Based on your qualification call, everything moves forward properly, or it gets hung up on issues that were not surfaced initially. This is truly an art, but it has some science to it as well. The important thing to keep in mind, is that you should *not* try to screen every candidate *into* your pipeline. The goal is to be generating solid candidates for your clients, so ideally, you are only putting deals into your pipeline that have a chance of closing. This means that you really should be screening out, most of the leads you generate. Just because someone says they have money and want to buy a business, doesn't make them worthy of your time. Complying with your process and meeting basic requirements for business ownership is what makes someone a viable candidate.

Time is the currency of this business and you must spend it wisely. Discerning who is actually worthy of your time and attention is the key to success. You have to make judgements about candidates, and decide who to work with, and who to send on down the road.

Engagement is the name of the game in franchising. The franchisors who know how to truly engage the candidate, are the ones who sell the most units every year. Watch carefully how a franchisor responds to your candidate, once you make a referral. This is usually a good indicator of how likely they are to close deals. The quicker, and more polished their response, the better they usually are at the rest of the discovery process too. If we are doing our jobs properly, this engagement starts with us and we can really help move the discovery process along. So from the beginning, we want to effectively set the table for the "first date" between our candidate and the franchisor.

Right from the start, I am brutally honest with each candidate. I explain that I am a recruiter, and that I represent a different slice of the marketplace than they will get from business brokers, so I can help them in a way that not many people can. I make clear to them that as a recruiter, I am not paid unless I listen very well and I make good matches, so they can see that our interests are compatible. I am courteous, but I ask tough questions and I do not accept blow-off answers. I educate the candidate along the way, but I always make the call about them. I am genuinely fascinated by people's stories, especially the ones who have previously owned businesses. After 30 years of working in staffing and franchisee recruiting, I have seen my share of business models. Even so, I learn new things about various businesses everyday from my candidates. I listen, I learn, and I praise where appropriate. People like to be acknowledged for their accomplishments, but only when it is sincere, and appropriate in the context of your discussion.

Any candidate who is less than forthcoming with the information you need, must be pressed. You can't help a candidate with only a piece of the puzzle, and you are not providing value to your franchise customers, if you continually offer poorly screened candidates. Additionally, you will burn out of this business quickly, because you will make a fraction of the placements that a disciplined recruiter will. Keep in mind that the candidates are usually treading on unfamiliar ground - especially the ones who pretend they know everything, they are usually the most ignorant ones of all.

When you encounter candidates who don't respect your process, they likely won't respect the franchisor's process either, so don't waste your time with them. I'm all for taking risks based on a hunch, but that should be the exception to the rule, not the norm. For the most part, you will want your candidates to conform to your process for best results. The beauty of having a robust lead generation strategy in place, is that you never feel bad about eliminating a candidate when you have several more fresh leads waiting to be called.

Candidates are conditioned to be suspicious of anyone on the phone or internet, so you need to quickly give them a reason to talk to you. Simply saying you can help with their franchise search is generally not enough. The candidate needs to see you as a serious and competent professional with value to offer. An important element of that, is maintaining control of your process. Some candidates are used to running roughshod over people, but don't let anyone do that to you. You must be in control of the relationship from the beginning.

Sometimes candidates are so impressed with themselves, they act like bullies. One time, I left a message for a lead and he had his secretary return my call to announce that he could talk now. Ok, fine. I asked him what he did, and he proceeded to yammer on for several minutes about his vast empire of business holdings. The businesses were impressive, but he was not, so I was thinking that he must have inherited most of it. When he finished his diatribe, he proceeded to declare how busy he was, and suggested that I needed to talk to his secretary now. I laughed out loud at his absurd suggestion. I told him that I couldn't help someone so self absorbed, and that he was not a good candidate for a franchise. I told the secretary that I was sorry she was in the employ of such an obtuse person and excused myself from the call. I admit that the apology to the secretary was a little snarky, but we all need a little catharsis from time to time, and he deserved it.

At any rate, some folks are simply jerks, but some people are just so used to ordering others around, they think they know what is best in all situations. Don't let this type get away with trying to control the process. Simply explain how things work, and tell them that there are no short cuts to excellence. Let them know if they want be in control of a process that produces suboptimal results, they can do that with a rookie broker, but not you. There are few things as powerful as the take away, so use it to your advantage early and often. Remember, the candidate has no value if they are just going to embarrass you and waste the customer's time. Don't ignore the signs of a bad candidate, or you will reap what you sow. Again, I am (almost) never rude about it, but I proactively decide who is worthy of my time and who isn't. When I tell a candidate that I cannot help them, I usually will send them links or information to help them in some way. It could be fun to simply dispense advice all day, but that isn't what we are paid for. We need to make successful placements in order to thrive, so we have to maintain high standards.

The candidates are typically going to learn a lot from you during the qualifying call. This helps them begin to trust your advice and ideas. Don't worry about sounding smart, or trying to impress the candidate with your resume. In the last 15 years, I think I have been asked twice about my background. This is about the candidate, not you. You will be judged on the results you produce, not your career history. Initially, the questions you ask are what will make the candidate gain or lose confidence in your abilities. Answers are easy. Good questions require insight. Most candidates are unaware of their ignorance, but when we start to ask prescient questions about their lifestyle objectives and resources, they quickly see that we understand what the real drivers are, and they begin to learn from us. That is the point where your relationship starts to blossom. The more we teach the candidate, the higher their confidence in us, and in themselves. Confidence is the key to action for most candidates, so this is paramount.

Additionally, there are pervasive misconceptions about franchises in the general public, so you want to educate people on the virtues of a franchised business model. You can do this in a conversation, and in some cases you will have to, but in general you should offer them a document that spells out the core benefits of a franchised business. This is very important information, because you need to dispel a lot of misinformation, and help them understand why a franchise works. I try to teach my candidates that the value of a franchise, is contained in the business model.

 A business model is a proven tool for making money, and *that* is a valuable thing indeed. It isn't easy to build a successful business model, so there is a very high fail rate for private startups, *and franchise systems*. Perfecting a business model is a lengthy and expensive process of trial and error, that most companies do not survive. So creating a successful business model is a very big deal.

Candidates should understand that a franchise is not a problem, it is a solution, one that has significant intrinsic value. Paying a franchise fee to get a reliable money making machine is a bargain. Here are some additional virtues that candidates should appreciate:

- Risk Mitigation. A franchise operation has a lower risk of failure than an independent business. This is because the machine has been built, tested, refined and proven to be effective.

- Efficient Distribution. Many great ideas for a product or service fail to succeed simply because the entrepreneur runs out of cash before figuring out how to deliver their product into the hands of a paying customer. Distribution is everything! With all due respect to the Golden Arches, they do not have the best hamburgers, but they can distribute them more effectively than any other player, by far. So, they win.

- Experience. The experience of the franchisor's management team boosts operational efficiency, and helps the organization avoid costly mistakes. Effective training systems are also more likely with experienced franchise leadership. Additionally, the franchisor has tremendous experience in their own industry, but even more importantly, they have already designed a training program to impart this knowledge to new franchisees. Candidates must understand that their sales and management skills represent their value, not specific industry knowledge (franchisors already have that in abundance, they are not looking for more from candidates).

- Purchasing power. Leveraging the combined buying power of the group allows franchise systems to negotiate the best prices for goods and services required to run the business.

- Brand identity. Established franchisors may already enjoy brand awareness in your market, but the quality of a business model has nothing to do with whether or not a candidate has ever heard of it. Franchise business models include brand development strategies for quickly, and efficiently building brand identity in new markets. You need more than a Starbuck's sign to field a coffee shop, right?

- Management Systems. Franchisors provide management assistance to franchisees in the areas of human resources, accounting, facilities management, etc. They also have specialized software to run these elements of the business. The franchisor also helps tremendously with legal compliance issues that can escape small business owners.

- Planning. Many franchisors help franchisees develop a business plan that includes the standard operating procedures established by the franchisor, and realistic goals for the business.

- Start-up assistance. The franchisor has a great deal of experience accumulated from helping its franchisees open new profit centers. They know how to launch new units efficiently, saving advertising dollars, preventing mistakes, and shortening the ramp up time to profitability.

- Marketing assistance. The franchisor develops professional advertising campaigns, or provides advice on how to develop effective marketing programs locally. Advertising can be very expensive, so knowing which venues to be in, and which types of ads to run is critical. Additionally, comprehensive sales training is part of each model, so franchises typically outperform mom and pop shops, as a result.

- Access to financing. It is much easier to obtain financing for a franchise than a private startup. Lenders are very familiar with the success rates of franchises and prefer them to private start ups.

The process of educating your candidate will continue until the deal is closed, but it is important to set the tone initially. Make sure they at least understand that they are investing in a business model, not a brand, and that they are only a candidate, until approved by the franchisor. They have to essentially interview for the opportunity while they evaluate it. If they understand that much, you will get a lot more out of your relationships.

My objective is to qualify the candidate as soon as possible, so I like to get it done on the first call whenever I can. I know that there is an argument for a slow and deliberate process, but I like to work with motivated people. My reasoning is that if this is a front burner issue for them, they will want to talk to me, because they are serious about doing something. The biggest fear that people have regarding their search, is that they will leave a stone unturned, and miss something big. If their search is truly important and timely, the candidate will want to talk to you, as long as you sound authoritative. Remember, you need to establish some credibility, build rapport, explain the process, and get to the qualifying questions. If it is untenable to talk right then, set an appointment for as soon as possible.

Some candidates really want to hear from an insider about what the "hot" franchises are or they want you to talk about specific models before you have qualified them. Don't. Again, if they won't follow your process, they are unworthy of your time. Dump them and run. It is a terrible waste of time to get into a discussion about franchises with an unqualified prospect, so never talk about franchise options until they are qualified. Remember, you are in control, unless you cede that control to the candidate, so don't do it!

Qualifying is about asking good questions, and listening to the answers. Let the candidate talk, but keep them on point. Some candidates tend to over answer every question, while others will under-answer. Make sure you get what you need though. If they dodge, come back with the same question until you are satisfied. There is no "diet" version of what we do. You need to know the same things about every candidate in order to do your job, so stay on point. Evaluate the answers to your questions and ask follow-up questions if appropriate. Remember to keep the tone conversational, and use your qualifying form every time to be sure you record all of the answers you need.

It's important to quickly impress on the candidate that you are serious, and that you can help them. They also need to know that it will be cost free, and relatively painless for them to find out what we have to say. Serious candidates will want to see what you can come up with. Use a script, be clear, and get to the point quickly. Be professional, but not too rigid. It should feel like you are talking to a neighbor or a colleague. Your qualifying questions are a great bonding opportunity, so make sure you add comments where appropriate (i.e., "You have an impressive resume."). Ask appropriate follow up questions and be interested in the information. If you are actually interested in your candidate's story, you will get a lot more information that you can use when it is time for the matching process.

My first question to each candidate is usually, "Are you currently looking for a business?". This may sound silly, but it is worth confirming before you spend too much time with anyone. As long as they say yes, explain what you do and tell the candidate that you want to understand their skills, goals and resources, so you can offer up some local matches. I find most people are eager to tell their story, so I like to start with asking them if they know what their objective is at this point. This is designed to be a very wide open question. It gives them an opportunity to start talking with no guard rails, which is good, but be sure to maintain control of the conversation. You are indeed building rapport at this point, but don't get too far off track. Your questions are the framework for your discussion, so stay on point, but by all means, keep it conversational. Stick to your questionnaire, but try not to sound like it.

Quite often we are dealing with voicemail, so when I do not get the candidate live on the phone, I will use an alternating series of three voice messages and three emails to announce my value to them. Keep it short and sweet on the first email and voice message, and get increasingly more detailed on your second and third attempts. By the third email and phone call, I have left zero question about who I am or what I want. If anyone doesn't respond to me, it isn't because they are unclear on what I do. Advertisers will tell you to call all of your leads at least ten times, or something like that. I don't. I may recycle the lead, and call it again later, but I do not chase leads. If finding a business is really important to the candidate, he will probably call me back. If I have to call a candidate seven times before he acknowledges me, I don't really want to work with someone like that. Do you?

Another tactic that has become popular lately is texting new leads, sometimes as the first point of contact. I kind of feel my age with this, like I do with social media. If you are someone who texts a lot, and you like the idea of it - go for it. Personally, I find unwanted text messages far more annoying than unwanted email, so I am not big on this strategy. Again, it may be just my age, so I don't want to discourage anyone who favors texting. If done properly, I am sure it can yield good results, but again you need to decide who you are trying to recruit and what methods suit you best.

Remember that depending on where, and how the candidate has been looking for information, they may be getting bombarded with calls, emails, and texts from multiple brokers and recruiters. Some candidates respond by ignoring everyone and hiding out for a month or so. If I exhaust my three calls and three emails, I put the lead in the cold file. These cold leads are put into a four month tickle file to start the process again (unless I am too busy, with current leads at that time). Sometimes people are just not ready yet, so it can be a good idea to try again after some time has passed.

When I do reach the candidate live on the phone, I start by telling them who I am and why I am calling them. For example, "This is Dan Brunell, I'm calling regarding your inquiry from X". Pause to let them focus, then ask, "Are you currently looking for business opportunities?".

If they say yes, but indicate that they only want to buy an existing business, I ask them why. Usually, they say they can't wait for a paycheck or they need immediate cash flow. A lot of people think it is safer to buy an existing business or that it is somehow easier, so they say that is all they want to see. It is important to remind these folks that, if their goal is to be in business for themselves, that is a long term play and a resale may or may not play to their best advantage. It is very competitive for resale businesses and they often come with issues that need to be fixed. Those issues often require more investment, so the cashflow that was showing under the previous owner can disappear when the business is being run by the book. I tell candidates that limiting yourself to only the businesses that are publicly available on the resale market, is like standing in an apple orchard and insisting on only picking up the apples that are already on the ground.

At this point, I ask them how their search is going. If they are relying on broker listings to find an acquisition, you know they are seeing a lot of problematic and overpriced businesses, so they are frustrated with the search process already. I ask them how much they are willing to invest. If it is 100k or more, I ask them if they would be interested in a start up opportunity for half that price. I tell them they could start building equity from day one, doing something they like, in a convenient location, and they can either pay themselves a salary or keep the other half of the investment dollars in the bank to live off while getting started. Almost anyone who is actually looking for a business will be interested in hearing what you have to say. If they say no, send your contact info, ask for a referral and move on. Don't sweat it, it is just a lead. Go get more!

If I proceed, I usually say something like; "Let me tell you what I do. I recruit owners for franchise systems with resale and new market opportunities. They pay me to find qualified owners for their franchises. What I do with Individuals, is to help clarify their objectives, and then execute a search to find options that line up with their qualifications and interests. I'll present my findings to you, and you tell me who you want to meet. Then I'll introduce you at a high level into the organization. It is up to you and the franchisor to fall in love or not. I will stay with you to help you through the discovery process, but I am not the sales guy, so I will stay neutral on the things we look at."

I then say, "I'd be happy to help you if you would like a fresh perspective". They typically say yes, so I say "Great, I just need to ask you some questions in order to set up the search parameters."

From there, proceed to your qualifying form and start asking your questions. Always use your qualifying form and write your notes on it, or type them directly into your CRM if you can. Most qualifying forms have the questions laid out in a specific sequence. The sequence should be designed to provide the needed information, but also to save time. The right questions help you eliminate people that are not ready or able to benefit from your help. I like to ask very early in the conversation, how soon they can act. You might ask, On a scale of 1 to 10 how important is it to find a business in the next 3 months? This question will really sort out the casual lookers. If they respond with anything less than seven, I tell them it is premature to search. I say that the landscape changes rapidly and if they are not ready to jump on opportunities and speak with people, they are not a good candidate for my help right now. Never feel bad about telling people that you can't help them, that is part of your job. Remember, be polite and offer to send them some resources that may help. Done. You need to extricate yourself from unworthy candidates as quickly as possible.

Make sure you help candidates clarify their goals if they are unclear at this point. Help them understand that each type of business will have a very specific implication on their lifestyle. Gain agreement on what it is that they really want their work week to look like. Help them arrive at a realistic and comfortable investment level. They will feel best about you if you help them to not overspend. I use the 50% or less of net worth equation. When they tell me their net worth, I suggest that they cut that number in half and use that as a not to exceed limit on their business investment. It is prudent to be conservative, but this also makes financing a no brainer later on.

Key Qualifying Questions

In order to make the most of your qualifying time with a candidate, it is best to always follow your form, but you want to be sure you ask a few important things up front. You must first establish that the candidate is looking for a business, and then ask what business they are in now to get the ball rolling, but very soon after that, you must assess how much of a priority this is for them. I like to ask things like:

- How important is it for you to find a business in the next few months?

- If we find a fit are you ready to speak with sellers?

- Once you find the right business, how soon do you wish to start?

These questions will give you a strong sense of how important this is to the candidate. If it is not a top priority for them, it shouldn't be for you either. I also like to assess whether or not a candidate is suited for b2b environments, or if b2c is better for their skill sets and preferences. There are a number of ways to address this, but it essentially comes down to whether or not they have sales and/or sales management skills. B2b businesses are driven by sales, whereas b2c businesses are driven by advertising. If someone is afraid of making sales calls or finds sales unpalatable, they should probably not be considering a b2b operation.

After those critical initial assessments, the crux of the qualification is going to focus on understanding their capabilities and lifestyle goals. Often candidates haven't developed these yet, so you need to help them figure out what is important, which is what your questionnaire should be designed to do. It amazes me how many people I talk to who have plans that are out of sync with their goals. It makes me feel good to at least get them on the the right path, by getting them to ask themselves the right questions. Clearly, this is a vital part of the conversation, and for some, it is the first time they have thought about the lifestyle implications of owning certain businesses. Once you have this defined, it is simply a matter of figuring out which environments are most conducive.

Clearly, this process has a strong funneling effect, so if you have a good sense of their qualifications and preferences, it makes the matching process pretty simple. Once you have completed your qualifying form, make sure you book a fixed appointment time to review your results with them. This is critical. They must respect that you are busy and that you are helping them, not the other way around. Always send an emailed appointment confirmation reminding them of the time and date. This is a good time to include information about the franchise discovery process, and the benefits of a proven business model too.

Chapter 5 - Matching Perspective

As stated in the previous chapter, the matching process should be fairly simple if you have adequately qualified the candidate. Additionally, if you specialize in recruiting for a given vertical market, like say food & beverage or residential services, your matching process will be more streamlined, because you only need to find the right match within that category.

You will want to give matching your best effort, because the candidate is not going buy something that isn't a fit for his objectives. You will likely surprise the candidate with your findings, so be prepared to help them understand why you selected that match for them. We shouldn't simply help people access businesses they were already targeting. We see a much bigger marketplace than prospective franchise buyers will ever see, so they do not have the benefit of knowing what is actually available to them. You need to share what you know, and apprise them of the hidden opportunities that they typically wouldn't have has access to. This is part of the huge value that we represent to the candidate. Knowing what questions to ask and where to find the answers, is what makes you an expert. Use your expertise to stop candidates from aimless wandering on the internet.

As stated above, our role is to lead people to certain options that are a fit, not to simply help them research their own ill-conceived ideas. Nonetheless, if the candidate really wants to learn about frozen yogurt, I will include that in my results, but I will also present two or three other options that I think are the right fit for them. The candidate's initial preferences are important, but keep in mind that their ideas and priorities are likely to change as they discover what things are most important to them, and what other types of businesses are actually available to them.

Before I begin a search, I like to do a little research on the candidate's home market area. There are great resources on-line, so you can do things like read the local paper, and get detailed demographic data for free. It really impresses the candidate if you know some things about their market, but it may also help you narrow down your potential picks for the candidate too. Your franchise customers are another great resource. I know a lot of the territory checks are handled via email now, but be different, call and check the territory in person. Ask the sales person what they know about the market. They may have some very key details that can help you (e.g., the number one franchisee in the system will be their neighbor), or they may know nothing, but it is worth asking.

As you know, when matching candidates to business opportunities, you are simply funneling down from hundreds of options into three or four. You can decide if you like to show only three, or if you think showing four concepts has merit, but never go past four at one time. It is far too much information, and for some, three will be a lot, so use your judgement.

While there are applications that can do some of the matching process for you, there is no substitute for your personal discretion. You know the marketplace, you know what the franchisors are looking for, and you know the candidate. Your intuition is the key ingredient in making the right match. At the end of the day, we are mostly matching to their lifestyle objectives, price range and skill set, so keep your focus on these elements.

When thinking about their skills, I always draw a line between whether they are a sales person or a non-sales person of course, but I also think about how receptive they will be to a new concept. During the course of filling in your qualifying questionnaire, you will usually get a feeling as to whether someone is more traditional or more cutting edge in their outlook. This will indicate whether or not they will be receptive to newer concepts that do not necessarily have an existing market, or will be better suited for something that has a strong demand already. Once we consider these factors and have a list of likely potential matches, the territory availability will usually pare our list down considerably. Sometimes, whatever is left over is all you can present.

The best way to be sure you are showing the right concepts to the candidate, is to refer back to the qualifying form, and take note of what their key criteria were. What were their lifestyle and financial objectives? What are they good at? Did they need to be close to home? Do they need flexible or family friendly hours? B2b or b2c? Price range? Earning potential? A quick review will help you determine what will work and what to avoid for the candidate as you consider potential options.

After the territory checks and my own analysis have trimmed the suspect companies down to my list of finalists, I consider more intangible criteria in order to finalize my list. Truth be told, I usually present four options, so if I have more than that, I go one by one through them to see which four are the closet match for the candidate's objectives. The key to good matches is finding the opportunities that support the lifestyle and financial objectives of the candidate. If you can match well to those two areas, you will delight your candidates more often than not.

Chapter 6 - Presenting Opportunities

Depending on what network you belong to, or who trained you initially, you are likely following a standardized procedure for presenting business concepts to candidates. If you have been at this for a while, I'm sure you have a solid process in place, but I'd like to offer a few pointers that seem to make a lot of difference.

First off, one of the biggest mistakes I made when I started my franchisee recruiting business, was giving the candidates too much credit. I thought that anyone contemplating a business would understand their net worth, and how loans work. I also thought that most candidates would understand the merits of a franchise, as long as I did a great job of explaining it. Boy was I wrong!

You can find a brilliant match, and flawlessly articulate how it supports their objectives, but some candidates simply won't see it. Of course, this can be an indication that you didn't qualify well enough, but even if you do everything perfectly, it can still fall flat because of the candidates emotional response to the idea. This is an excellent reason not to get too invested in any of the businesses you present. Your best interests are usually served by remaining somewhat neutral. If a candidate warms to any particular concept, and I genuinely have enthusiasm for the company, I certainly will share that information, but I try not to steer them too much. I am always delighted if they like any of my picks, as long as they like at least one of them enough to want an introduction. Our mission is simple, create an appetite for more information.

Most candidates have never owned a business before, so they are on unfamiliar ground. Additionally, many candidates have their heads filled with half truths, and faulty assumptions about franchises and business ownership in general. And again, most candidates are more driven by emotion than analysis. Given these truths, I've developed some strategies to quickly educate my candidates and facilitate more productive exchanges.

After the qualifying call, I always email the candidate an appointment confirmation that includes key information on franchising, and what to expect in the process. I start the presentation call by referring back to the information that I sent after our last call. This gives me a chance to take control of the conversation and further prep them before we start. I like to highlight the value of the discovery process and specifically, I like to discuss the value of the validation calls that they will ultimately make. I tell the candidate that the franchisors are a great source of information, but they will only get good news and sunshine from the franchisor. I let them know that the franchisees will share the good, the bad, and the ugly during validation, so these are crucial calls to make in order to evaluate their fitness for the model.

I like to explain that the purpose of validation is essentially to confirm that what the franchisor has told them is accurate. I let them know that the distribution of results normally looks like a bell curve. Some are doing exceedingly well, and others are failing, but most are somewhere in the middle. I want to help manage their expectations, because if they think they are supposed to witness perfection and happiness across the board, they won't survive the validation process. I tell them that if 90% of a franchise system's units are successful, there is nothing wrong with the business model. The 10% that are failing is a result of user error, not a bad franchise. I also tell them that this is the best way to get a read on what their upside potential is going to look like, irrespective of what Item 19 says.

I discuss the value of competent counsel when reviewing franchise documents. I explain to them that when they are ready to invest, the FDD and agreement should be read by an experienced franchise attorney who represents buyers, not franchisors. I also explain why and what the downside of using a bad attorney could be. Early on, I learned this the hard way. When I first started my business, I met a local attorney through a networking group. He wanted my referrals, so he over-represented his level of experience with franchise law. I fell for it, and sent him a local candidate. To make a long story short, the candidate unfortunately paid far too much for representation by someone to whom, I had to ultimately explain franchise law. Some brokers prefer to keep their candidates away from attorneys, but a good recruiter knows that the candidate will likely seek help, with or without your advice, so it is better to be sure they are getting competent help. Again, it is a good practice to always be compiling lists of professionals in the markets where you work, they will come in handy.

After those key points are covered, I start the presentation by recapping their core objectives. I restate what they told me during the qualifying call to remind them of what their stated goals were.

Sometimes you have to highlight the bullseye, so they know when you hit it. This also allows you to learn if anything has changed now, instead of at the end of your presentation. Once you have agreement that the objectives are correct, then proceed with your presentation.

Regarding the concepts that we select for the candidate, we usually have some intuitive feeling about which options will be best for the candidate. Remember not to get too invested in any of your choices. There is some debate in our business about the optimal order in which to present your franchise selections. Is it best to lead with your strongest option or to hold that one until the end? I don't think it is crucial, but as I mentioned, I usually present four options and I like to start with my second favorite, then present my third best, follow that with my favorite option, so it is in the middle, and then last is usually the weakest one. The weakest option is often the idea that they thought they would want to pursue initially, before they had a better read on their objectives. Again, I don't know how much difference it really makes, because ideally all of your picks should be a decent match in order to make the final cut. Nonetheless, it always makes for a smoother presentation when you plan the order of the selections ahead of time. It can help lead the candidate to the best conclusion too. The contrast of the last two options that you show the candidate (strongest match vs. weakest) helps them appreciate the stronger match more.

Clearly the purpose of the presentation is to show the candidate businesses that support his objectives, but *your* goal is to create enough interest within the candidate to speak with at least one of the franchisors you present. I think it is important to stay at a high level when presenting each company. Giving the candidate the highlights is enough at this point. Let them ask questions, and briefly share what you know, but always be encouraging them to speak with the franchisor. The reality is that until our candidate is engaged with a franchise customer, we aren't even in the vicinity of making a deal happen. Everything we do, needs to be focused on getting our candidates to speak with solid potential matches.

At the end of the presentation the only question for the candidate should be about which companies he wants to speak with. I usually have them rank them in terms of initial interest and then tell them that we will focus on the top two. I will give the candidate a heads up on what to expect and who will be reaching out to them. I then follow that up in an email with the link to the franchisor's website, and some questions they should ask. I do not want the end of the presentation to be a discussion about whether or not they want to talk to any of the companies, only which one(s). When you initially qualified the candidate, you gained their consent to speak with the companies that were a fit, so hold them to it. This is critical to your success, so make sure you set the stage properly during your qualifying call. Candidates need to understand that no proprietary information will be shared with them until they have a successful conversation with a human from the franchisor.

If you show the candidate four concepts that match his goals, and he doesn't think any of them are compelling enough to speak with, you have failed in your mission. The candidate is saying that he is not ready to take your word that this is worthy of his time. If they say, "I want to look at the websites" or "do some research" before they are willing to engage with the franchisor, you did not explain the process well, or you didn't make a compelling argument about the franchise offering. If I get pushback at this point, I am very candid with them. I tell them the websites only show front facing public information, and the pertinent, proprietary information is not available on the internet or among their friends. I reiterate why I selected the company as a match for them, and remind them that if they are not talking to humans, they are not gathering the information that they really need. Tell them you will send the website links, but they need to have a chat with your client in order to learn what they need to know.

I'll share with the candidate that in a brief conversation with a franchisor, they will both learn whether or not this is worthy of investing further time. I want them to understand that the franchisor may choose not to advance them as a candidate. Why spend a ton of time trying to piece together an external analysis that provides zero illumination of the actual business model? Especially if you may not even be approved. If we prepare the candidate from the start to treat this like a job interview process, they will understand that the analysis starts only after the initial contact with the franchisor. Until then, everything else is third party information, which is notoriously unreliable, and can be more confusing than illuminating.

Use your standardized form every time you make a referral. After you email the referral to the client company, follow it up with a phone call. You want to be sure that the franchise sales person has received your candidate's information, but you also want them to know that you are a serious referral agent who is going to work with them to get the candidate through the discovery process.

Be prepared to deal with fear. Candidates will have rational, and irrational fears. Fear is not unusual, and it isn't necessarily bad, but it needs to be put into context. If someone is truly paralyzed by fear, they are probably not a great candidate to own a business, but normal fears and even mild apprehensions, can stop a person from moving forward too. Fear is an indication that tells us we are worried about losing something. That is a natural defense mechanism, but it can be a powerful motivator for action or inaction. Sometimes, just telling a candidate that a little fear is healthy and normal, is enough to get them past it. In any case, it is something you should address, because it can be deadly to your deals.

Chapter 7 - Pipeline Management

Once you have introduced your candidate to the franchisor, and they have engaged, it is important to stay close, but not be overbearing. I like to try to set the ground rules with my candidates during the qualifying call, and I reiterate the rules of engagement in the written materials that I share with them. I want the candidate to know that I am available to them, but I want them to understand that the discovery process is where they need to focus. I explain that it is unique to each franchisor, and they need to embrace it if they want to make the best decisions about their future. I like to have at least weekly contact once someone is in my funnel, but I will alternate my touches between email and phone calls, (and sometimes, yes, I send text messages if appropriate).

Debriefing the Candidate

After the initial conversation with the franchisor, the candidate will have some impressions about the company. I don't use a set list of questions at this point, I mostly listen and probe where needed. You mostly want to find out if they are ready to continue learning about the opportunity, and if any red flags surfaced. It is important to be a part of the feedback loop if you want to remain relevant in the process too. I always want my franchise customers to feel like they are getting continuing value from me throughout the process. I like to be able to tell the customer about my candidate's thoughts, so they can address any issues, or reinforce any specific information.

I do not sit in on meetings or arrange conference calls, but I always follow up with my candidates after their franchisor calls. I also follow up with the franchisor after each call, unless they reach me first. The best franchise sales people let you know every time they interface with your candidate, but you can groom all of your customers to do this if they know you will always be calling them anyway.

It is important to make sure that the candidate and the franchisor are communicating effectively. I am often amazed at how two people can interpret the exact same conversation totally differently, so don't leave things to chance. You can contribute tremendously to the closing process by sharing pertinent information with the franchisor on a timely basis. The candidate will tell you things that they won't tell the franchisor, and vice versa, so you need to communicate.

I always underscore to candidates, that these are my customers and I don't want anyone to make me look bad. Again, there's no excuse for bad manners! I tell them that as a referred candidate, the franchisor assumes they are technically qualified, but that doesn't guarantee their access to the franchise opportunity. They have to be awarded the opportunity to buy the franchise, so it is far from being a given. What the franchisor is looking for is professionalism and likability, because they are selecting a business partner. It isn't a transaction, it is more like a marriage, so candidates should be reminded of that early and often.

If the candidate has been paying attention at all, they know that I don't expect much from them, other than a little professionalism. That usually manifests itself in prompt communication. The candidate doesn't have to report their every move to me, but I do expect to be in loop. I make it easy for them by calling and emailing each week so they have two ways to respond. When I email, I like to include an interesting news article or a resource that they can use. This makes it a little less like they are simply reporting to you and it gives you an opportunity to continue to add value for the candidate.

Now that you have the candidate in the pipeline, your mission is to go get more! Keep putting quality deals into your funnel everyday, and you will eventually have a consistent revenue stream. Rinse and repeat (ad nauseam).

Customer Service

You should always be looking for ways to help each of your franchise customers move the deals along. Some companies are very adroit at moving candidates through the discovery phase, while others basically let the candidate control the process. One of the things I like to do, is to remind the candidate that they need to be pursuing the money to fund the deal before they get too deep into a discovery process. I also remind them to connect with a franchise attorney or other appropriate professionals as needed. I always send them information on funding programs and offer to refer them to competent professionals who can help as well. I also like to ask them about their calendar availability for a discovery day visit, after they have logged a couple of positive calls with the franchisor. I want them thinking about this early, and often. They need to know that discovery day is the final step in evaluating a franchise partner and it is where we are heading, unless they want to step off the train. Sending them questions to ask, other materials about discovery day or financing options, etc., can keep them moving forward and keep this process top of mind in their day to day lives.

Sometimes we can help the franchisor simply by educating the candidates more about the marketplace in general, or how small businesses accomplish certain functions, etc. There is no shortage of things for a new business owner to know, so you can always be sharing pertinent information with the candidate. I have trained a lot of people to be franchisee recruiters over the years, and one thing that I've told every one of them, is to start a drip feed file and always be on the lookout for content. Any article that could be of interest to a small business owner or prospective franchisee should be added to the file. If you are doing your reading, you cannot help finding content. Whether the article is about funding sources or motivating employees, it doesn't matter. Just always be adding to the drip file, and you will be sure to have plenty of content to share. If you see an article that any of your franchise customers might like, clip it and send it to them. Being just a little bit thoughtful will set you apart and make customers remember you.

Another way to help the franchisor is to make sure that questions get asked and answered. Sometimes deals get derailed because the candidate makes assumptions that are completely false. It is important to be talking to the candidate, so that these questions come up. Especially if there is something negative, like a complaint on the internet, it is good to get these cleared up sooner rather than later. If I am asked about something like that, I say, "Not sure, but I think that is a great question to ask Phil when you speak again. Often, internet complaints are from people who have an axe to grind, legit or not. I don't think you should ignore any input about things that went wrong, but I'd be a lot more interested in talking to some of their successful franchisees to see if you can replicate what they are doing right. Does that makes sense?". This will allow for the concern to be addressed, and it educates them that there may be other reasons driving someone's bad review of the company.

The key thing to remember in customer relationships, is to be professional. If you can produce excellent candidates, the customers will truly appreciate you for that alone. However, if you are thoughtful and helpful, they will love you. It only takes a tiny bit more effort to be above average, so make that choice and go the extra mile for your customers. We are all trying to help our customers save time and money, while avoiding headaches, so remember your role, and make these things your mission. Remember that your relationship with the franchise sales person is critical, but the franchisor is your customer, and you can protect your customer's interests by respecting their time, even when their own sales staff may not. I cut off chatty franchise sales people all the time. I love energetic, and enthusiastic franchise sales professionals, but I want them spending their time and energy with my candidates, not me.

Most franchisors have an expectation that the candidate will complete the discovery process within a certain time line. For some companies that could be as little as 30 days and for others, it could take 3 or 4 months. In any case, there has to be an effort made to close the sale. Ideally, this effort shouldn't be coming from us. We can help, but we are not the sales people in this equation, and we have no authority to make an award offer or receive an acceptance. The franchise sales person must take deliberate action to bring the process to an end. At some point, the candidate must continue to advance or die. That usually means committing to a discovery day visit or not. If they can't commit, they need to be removed from the process until they are ready to either say no to that company, or finish the last step.

At the end of the discovery process, which is usually an in person meeting with the franchisor, an award must be extended or not, and the candidate needs to accept or not, ideally within a few days of the award. Typically, the candidate has decided before they leave discovery day, so if they say they need time to think it over, what they are really saying is, I want to make sure there are no better offers close at hand before I say yes to this one. That is not a great position to be in, so if your candidate needs to think about things, ask them what things? Don't be pushy, but be frank. Tell them that you have been at this a long time, and it seems that everyone has the same concerns. Tell them that you can likely shed some light on whatever questions they have or at least tell them where they can get further information. Again, sometimes it helps the candidate if he knows that it is ok to be a little scared. A little fear is a healthy thing, it keeps you alert and thinking. That is a big difference from the debilitating fear that consumes some candidates once they learn about the commitments that business owners make. Hopefully, you won't have many of those slip by you, but you need to pay attention to their responses during qualifying and make sure you are satisfied that they have the right stuff.

Sometimes we need to coach our customers along too, so don't be afraid to offer some information on how you have seen other companies overcome obstacles (like closing sales!). I am not suggesting you share proprietary information, but these franchise sales people know that we have a very good read on the marketplace, and many will appreciate your input. Some of them will even try to pump you for direct information on their competitors, so be careful about what you share with whom, and don't break any restrictive covenants you are bound by.

Sometimes the franchisor's discovery process can have certain aspects that appear awkward to us, or the company's marketing materials can have a mistake or typo. Feel free to discuss any trouble spots that you see with your clients. Always do so in the spirit of continuous improvement. Don't be rude or judgmental about it, just politely share your thoughts. If you are polite about it, you don't need to worry about offending the client. If the client embraces your feedback and appreciates the suggestion, you know you have a good client relationship. If they don't want to hear it or refuse to act on good advice, then you know this is a company that you should probably not get too invested in.

Building on a good relationship and turning it into a great relationship, is really about going above and beyond minimum expectations. If you look at each of your favorite customers, you can see that they all have some very specific objectives on their plate at any given time. Always ask your customers about their mission objectives. Understand what they are trying to accomplish, and then help them get there. I of course, always ask about their key target markets. You should know the top three targets for all of your favorite customers, and you should be working to fill them in. This business is so much more fun when you are recruiting for the companies you really like. It certainly feels good and it can be quite rewarding financially, to be a part of their goal attainment. For soloists like us, being considered part of our customer's team, can be very gratifying and make this job a little less lonely.

What I have found is that the franchise development staff usually have a territory or two stuck in their craw for some reason. Maybe they were really close after months and months of work, and the deal fell through. This is a common occurrence and you will find that if you ask, you will receive plenty of information on these sore spots. I make these my top target markets to recruit in, because I know that all of the workup on these markets is done and that the franchisors are chomping at the bit to close deals there. Even if you are unknown to a new franchise customer, this method will ensure that your candidates are the top priority for the sales group.

If you identify the biggest challenge that your customer has, and figure out how to help them fix it, you will be rewarded far beyond your fees. When you go about offering specific assistance to help your clients resolve problems, you are no longer a vendor, you become a key contributor. It is no surprise that a lot of franchisee recruiters are hired by the franchisors who come to find them indispensable.

Franchisee recruiting can be a very rewarding business. It certainly can make a big difference in the lives of the candidates we work with, and the organizations that we help grow. We have a positive influence on the markets we serve, and the economy in general. The franchise industry provides vital jobs, as well as goods and services that keep our world going everyday. In other words, you are a key part, of a critical element, in the broader schema (I think I will put that on my next batch of business cards). I hope you have found some of this information helpful. If you are able to get even one more deal per year with these tips, it will be worth the read, but I hope you are able to do much more than that with this information. I wish you the best of luck in your franchisee recruiting business!

Made in the USA
Middletown, DE
11 March 2020